A Calendar of Cotswold Cookery

June Lewis-Jones

SIGMA Leisure

Originally published as *The Cotswold Cook Book* by Cotswold Life Limited in 1990

Published by Sigma Leisure – an imprint of
Sigma Press, Stobart House, Pontyclerc, Penybanc Road
Ammanford, Carmarthenshire SA18 3HP
www.sigmapress.co.uk

British Library Cataloguing in Publication Data

A CIP record for this book is available from the British Library

ISBN: 978-1-85058-873-3

Typesetting and Design by: Sigma Press, Ammanford, Carmarthenshire

Photographs: June Lewis-Jones

Cover photographs: June Lewis-Jones

Printed by: Akcent Media Limited

This collection is dedicated to my husband, Ralph and my colleagues at *Cotswold Life*

Contents

Introduction

My interest in cooking came at the early age of discovering Granny Lewis's larder. The larder at Coneygre Cottage in the Coln Valley was a cool and cavernous store-room of pots and crocks, jugs and jars, barrels and baskets and bottles and boxes: a place of sweet-smelling shadows which took on familiar forms as one got accustomed to the half-light permitted through the wire gauze which covered the small window. The larder was a place of wonder, a veritable treasure-house where the harvest of farm and field and hedgerow and Gramp's garden was stored. It was a silent, secret place; a place into which I crept just to look and wonder, with the same reverence as reserved for church and Great Aunt Annie's front parlour, equally as timeless and awe-inspiring.

To have bustled in, flooding it with light would have shattered the magic of the larder. And magical it was. Within those lime-washed knobbly stone walls, bulging and bristling with chunky necklaces of golden-skinned onions and prickly with pungent bunches of herbs, some metamorphosis transformed the glazed-eyed hare, whose cold fur my little fingers had tentatively touched, sending delicious shivers of terror down my spine, into the hot and heady hot-pot; a huge tongue, as from some prehistoric monster, come upon unexpectedly soaking up the water in Granny's rose-patterned handbowl, became the creamy pink slices in her brown bread sandwiches.

The larder, while seemingly caught in a time warp, was a place of transition: things were always at different stages in the larder; muslin bags hanging from cup hooks on the edge of the paper-lined shelves were draining curds from whey; game was hanging, mincemeat was maturing, and Gramp's wine 'worked' in the earthenware crocks, while Granny's pastry 'rested' above on the marble slab.

Yet, despite this seemingly endless period of waiting there was always a plentiful round of pies and puddings and wedges of cake, dishes of jams and junkets, and jugs of wine and cordials which appeared on the table as if by magic. The secrets of what could be conjured up from the depths of the larder were recorded and kept on the corner shelf in small black leather bound notebooks, bulging with crumpled edged scraps and notes and cuttings, culled from friends and neighbours, ladies' journals and the church monthly magazine. The receipts and wrinkles read like some ancient alchemy practice — the secret key to unlock the door to the old-fashioned delights of Granny Lewis's larder.

I still am a compulsive reader of receipts — as recipes were always called. I scan the long lists of ingredients, hungry to get to 'the method' with all the thrill and anticipation of a medieval who-dunnit. My magpie mind searches for the reason why this dish was so named and why that cake was baked on special occasions. And this book is the result. My family is rooted in the rich red soil of the Cotswold's since, it seems, time began, so it is with an almost primeval spirit that I feel the affinity with the seasonal cycle of seedtime and harvest, and the reason for celebrating our rich heritage of festivals with traditional fare. It is this continuity with our past that is so richly rewarding to the present, yet in the process of progress we are in danger of losing so much of those simple pleasures of creation — and that is what cooking is — a creativity of preparation and judgement and skill to satisfy a basic human need. We have to eat to live, so it might as well be a pleasure. There is a lot of love goes into cooking and it is the best way I know to show someone that you care: I take it as an enormous compliment if my host or hostess produces a homely home-cooked meal for me; equally I take as one of my endearing compliments that as I am writing this I have received a letter from a publisher in Lancashire — the home of good cooks — saying, and I quote: 'I often mention to people up here, the splendid lunch you gave me some years ago ... it was a happy meeting'. The lunch was eight years ago! And was a simple affair, but everything was home-baked from home-grown food.

This book then, is a collection of good old-fashioned cookery. There are no fancy quiches or gateaux, sweets or desserts — but plenty of puddings, dunch dumps and pies. Such odd names as might appear belong to the region — these were the names by which the old dishes were known by those who cooked and ate them long ago. I feel it is as important to record those lovely old dialect words, with their rhythmic syllables and colourful cadence, as the receipts for the Cotswold fare.

Regional dishes do, of course, stem initially from the kind of produce which can be produced locally and much could be written on the salmon fishing and the elver catch peculiar to the Severn, the Double Gloucester cheese from the lush Vale and the apple-flavoured pork of the Gloucester Old Spot, from centuries of scrumping apples in the orchards; of the beautiful trout that tantalise fishermen in their season, the game-stocked coveys and wood-fringed fields where hares lollop along and rabbits scurry away; of the slow-growing barley on the stone-brash Wolds and the cottage gardens where beans tumble in tresses from coppice poles and pot marigolds splash colour among the carrot tops. The magic of my childhood memories of the larder are all there — flying, swimming, grunting, growing and greening in the countryside. Each in their season — just as it says in the Scriptures. It is the seasons, and the delight each brings by way of fruitfulness or festivity, special to my beloved Cotswolds, that are the warp and weft of this fabric of food and how to enjoy it the old-fashioned way.

June Lewis-Jones

Conversion Rates

imperial	metric
¼ pint	150 ml
½ pint	275 ml
¾ pint	425 ml
1 pint	570 ml
1½ pints	850 ml
2 pints	1.2 litre
3 pints	1.7 litre
4 pints	2.25 litre
5 pints	2.9 litre

½ pint is roughly equal to 1 American measuring cup, breakfast cup, mug or 2 gills

¼ pint is roughly equal to 1 English tea cup or 1 gill

7 tablespoons (serving spoons) water are roughly equal to ¼ pint

imperial	metric
½oz	10g
1oz	25g
2oz	50g
3oz	75g
4oz	110g
5oz	150g
6oz	175g
8oz	225g
10oz	275g
12oz	350g
16oz	450g
1lb	450g
2lb	900g
3lb	1.35kg
4lb	1.80kg
5lb	2.25kg

oz — ounce lb — pound
g — gram(s) kg — kilogram

January

First Day, Twelfth Night Poughshares and Distaffs

— Old Customs for a New Year

January takes its name from the Roman god Janus, derived fromthe Latin word for opening. As the New Year opened the first day was celebrated by giving presents, a custom which lasted in England until the Stuart period. Elizabeth I regularly received a pair of new gloves on each New Year day of her reign. The Wychwood Forest, on the eastern edge of the Cotswolds, provided the finest doeskin for the royal gift and the glovers of Woodstock stitched them into exquisitely cuffed and embroidered gloves.

An earlier queen is honoured at Oxford, where Queen's College is named after Queen Philippa, wife of Edward III, but the New Year's custom which has survived there is the needle and thread ceremony. This is a rebus on the name of Robert de Eglesfield, the founder. The Bursar hands a threaded needle to the Fellows on New Year's Day and bids them 'Take this and be thrifty'.

It is extraordinary that such a significant date, the first day of a new year, was allowed to lapse for so long before it was officially recognised again in 1972 as a Bank Holiday in England. But the apparent disregard for January 1st as a cause for celebration and wishing good luck for the coming year, was probably as a result of the confusion created by the English keeping March 25th as New Year's Day — all in accordance with the old Julian calendar, an accumulation of extra minutes and seconds which the introduction of the Gregorian calendar in 1582 had rectified in Catholic Europe, but which Protestant England refused to accept until 1752! Therefore, the old customs which have come down to us for the new year are on Old Christmas Eve, January 5th, the eve of Twelfth Night on the 6th. And this is where we start the year of festive food, traditionally prepared and served to celebrate the Cotswold calendar.

Wassailing the Apple Trees on Twelfth Night

Wassailing the apple trees, a custom which has lasted nearly a thousand years, has not completely died out, and in parts of the West Country a merry party armed with shotguns and horns and a pail of cider assemble in the orchard and toast the prime tree. This is carried out with a great deal of ritual: the lowest boughs may be brought down to dip into the cider pail if they can be reached; a piece of toast is soaked in the cider and laid in the crook of a branch, then the cider is poured round the base of the tree. Shots are fired and horns sound clear in the Twelfth Night wintery air, then the wassail song is sung. Each area has its own version, but this one is perhaps the most widely remembered:

Here's to thee, old apple tree,
Whence thou may'st bud and
whence thou may'st blow,
And whence thou may'st bear
apples enow.
Hats full, caps full, bushel, bushel
sacks full,
And my pockets full too! Hurrah!

As the blessing to the tree finished to ensure a good crop that year, the wassail bowl is handed round and the toast is drunk. Toasting the health of someone — or apple trees, in this case, actually springs from the ancient custom of placing toasted bread in the wassail bowl itself to add nourishment and decoration to it. Today, it is more usual to add toasted small apples for a traditional wassail bowl, and the apples again are symbolic of the purpose of 'toasting' the fruit trees. The word wassail comes down the centuries from the Anglo-Saxon term: waes hael — 'be healthy, or good health'.

Twelfth Night Cake

Twelfth Night ends the Yuletide festivities, and was once a robust occasion of great feasting and merriment, tomfoolery and mummery. A Lord of Misrule, a kind of Master of Ceremonies, was appointed to lead the junketings of the entire festive period, and held his final 'Court' on Twelfth Night, when a King of the Bean and a Queen of Marrowfat (Pea) would preside in state over the programme of dancing and feasting. The mock monarchs were selected purely by chance; the finder of the bean in the Twelfth Night cake became King and the one who found the pea became Queen. If the pea is found first by a man then he can choose his queen; likewise, if a lady finds the bean first then she elects who shall be her king. Emma Dent of Sudeley Castle at Winchcombe, wrote in 1890 of "the good times we had over the Twelfth Cake ..." The Twelfth Night cake is traditionally flatter than the normal fruit cake, but is iced and decorated, so is still a celebration cake.

Distaff Day and Plough Monday

Partly worke and partly play
Ye must on St Distaff's day
From the Plough soone free your teame;
Then come home and fother them
If the maides a spinning goe.
Burn the flax, and fire the towe;
Scorch their plackets, but beware
That ye singe no maiden-hire.
Bring in pails of water then,
Let the Maides bewash the men,
Give St Distaff all the right,
Then give Christmas sport good-night,
And next morrow, every one
To his own vocation

Herrick gives us a good description of the final holiday to mark the end of the Christmas season. Distaff Day was the time for the women to return to their spinning wheels immediately following Twelfth Night, whereas the men did not return to the plough until the first Monday following Twelfth Night — the actual return, though, was on the Tuesday, because Plough Monday, in turn, had first to be celebrated. Young farmworkers would rise early on Plough Monday, and the first to stake his claim to a fowl for the Shrovetide pot did so by placing his plough whip or staff by the farmer's kitchen fire, a sort of bonus for 'clocking in first'. After a couple of hours of the necessary 'fothering' of the team horses, the ploughmen bedecked their plough with ribbons and hauled it through the village to the accompaniment of the local Morris dancers and drum and pipe. Collecting money as they went on their merry way, maintained a 'Plough Light' to burn in the church to ensure good luck for the coming year's harvest.

The ancient custom has survived in subdued form in some places still where Plough Sunday services are held and a ploughshare is blessed. The most popular pub fare today is still the 'ploughman's', so it is close to tradition that I start the new year as a tribute to those sturdy sons of the soil and the spinsters who worked at the distaff and dishes. In any case, there is much to be said for the good old-fashioned country meal of hearty soup, crusty home-baked bread with cheese and tasty pickles — one dark and spicy, the other sweet and nutty.

A Twelfth Night cake, spiced beef, old-time puddings, a wassail bowl and the oldest drink known to those early Cotsallers bring a taste of the past to the present.

Country Spinner' Soup

2 carrots
2 onions
2 turnips
2 pints good beef stock
1 oz cornflour
1 oz clean dripping (or butter)
1 bay leaf
small bunch of parsley and thyme, chopped finely
seasoning

Prepare vegetables. Melt dripping (or butter) in large pan and add the onions, thinly sliced; soften until golden brown. Remove from heat and drain off excess fat. Add the rest of the vegetables, roughly chopped, the stock, herbs and seasoning to taste. Bring to the boil then simmer for 1 hour. Remove bay leaf. Sieve or liquidise. Make a thin paste of the cornflour with 2 tablespoons of water and stir in to thicken. Return to the pan. Simmer — but do not allow to boil again —for 10 minutes. Serve piping hot with hunks of freshly baked bread.

Ragoo of Mushrooms

(Adapted from an eighteenth century recipe)

(Serves 3-4)
12 ozs mushrooms (wild ones are best at the right time of year)
4 fl ozs full-bodied red wine (claret, if possible)
2 level tablesps flour
4 teasps each of grated nutmeg and mace
4 ozs butter
6 eggs

Put the eggs into a pan of cold water and bring to the boil. Boil for ten minutes while you prepare the rest of the dish, then run the hot eggs under cold water and crack the shells to prevent further cooking, but keep warm until assembling the ragoo. Sort the mushrooms, keeping 8 small ones aside, prepare and break off the stalks, chop them and add with the prepared mushrooms to a pan with a shake of salt and 4 tablespoons of the wine, cover and simmer gently until the mushrooms are softened. Add the rest of the wine and 3 ozs of the butter, toss gently to coat the mushrooms. Mix the flour and spices together and sprinkle over. Stir gently to blend and simmer over a low heat until the sauce thickens. While doing this, skin and take the stalks from the rest of the mushrooms, place a flake of the remaining butter inside each cap and grill under a low heat until softened. Shell the eggs and cut cleanly in half. Place in the centre of a warmed serving dish. Spoon the ragoo round the eggs, and finish with an outside ring of the grilled mushrooms. Serve at once.

Quick Cream Of Chicken Soup

(Serves 4)
½ lb cooked chicken (or any other poultry will do)
1 small onion
1 pint chicken stock
1 oz butter
1 tablesp parsley, finely chopped
1 rasher of bacon
¼ pint cream

Melt the butter in a large pan. Grate the onion and add to the butter with the rasher of bacon, snipped into small pieces; fry together for about 5 minutes. Add stock and bring to the boil. Simmer for 10 minutes. Remove the bacon — reserve to garnish. Add the cooked chicken and bring just to boiling point, skim off any excess fat. Remove from the heat and add cream, stirring to blend, keep over low heat while preparing the warmed soup dishes. Serve at once, sprinkled with the bacon pieces and the parsley.

Week-Spiced Beef

The name is taken from the length of time it takes for the beef to be spiced; therefore make sure you start preparing it in plenty of time before you intend to use it. This is derived from a recipe which dates back at least three centuries, when long spicing was essential to keep meat before refrigerators were invented. Nevertheless, even today, the lengthy process of spicing is worth the little trouble — there are no adequate shortcuts to achieve the same flavour, but I have omitted the saltpetre process, thus reducing the preparation by a few days.

3 lb silverside of beef
4 ozs brown sugar
1 oz black peppercorns
½ oz allspice
1 oz juniper berries
½ tablesp coarse salt

(Crush the peppercorns and juniper berries just before using). Wipe the meat and place in a stoneware (or glass) dish. Divide all the spices and sugar in half. Mix one half quantity with the salt and rub well into the beef, turning it over so that all sides are well covered, cover and leave in a cool place — preferably the fridge for 2 days. Remove from the spiced brine and rinse under cold water. Dry thoroughly with a clean cloth. Mix the remaining half quantity of sugar and spices together. Have ready a double thickness of foil large enough to wrap the meat in. Rub the mixed sugar and spices into the beef and wrap tightly in the foil. Leave in the fridge for a further 3 days, turning the package over a couple of times.

Cook, without unwrapping the beef, in a baking tin in a slow oven 140°C (Gas Mark 1) for 6 hours. Remove from the tin, but still keep wrapped. Turn the package over and place in a dish and while still hot, press under a pastry, or bread board with an old-fashioned fire-iron on top (or you can use a heavy bag of sugar as the weight). Leave overnight to get quite cold.

Beef, spiced in this way will have a delicious thin jelly coating and will keep, wrapped in its cooking wrappers, for at least a week in the fridge although I doubt whether there will be much left by that time! Even the scraps and scrapings can be used up as a tasty spread in sandwiches or on toast.

Bacon and Apple Hot Pot

(Serves 4)
1½ lb collar of bacon
2 tablesps oil
1 level tablesp cornflour
½ pint dry cider
¾ pint stock
1 level teasps tomato puree
2 eating apples
black pepper

Leave the bacon to soak in cold water overnight to remove excess salt. Drain and cut into 1½ inch sized cubes. Heat the oil in a large pan and fry the bacon pieces for about 5 minutes. Stir in the cornflour, then gradually add the stock and cider and puree, stirring to avoid lumps. Season with pepper. Bring to the boil, reduce the heat and keep at simmering point for about 45 minutes. Wash the apples and remove the cores, but do not peel, slice into fairly thick wedges, and add to the hot pot. Cook for a further 15 minutes to soften the apples. Serve with jacket or creamed potatoes.

It looks attractive if you have one green-skinned apple and one red-skinned for this dish. The addition of peanuts with the apples (about 2 ozs) adds a nice crunchy texture, but if the nuts are salted they need to be rinsed well first.

Chicken Cobbler

(Serves 4)
2 chicken joints
4 ozs mushrooms
1½ ozs butter
½ pint milk
¼ pint water
1 chicken stock cube
1 teasp lemon juice
10 ozs plain flour
2 teasps baking powder
3 ozs margarine
parsley to garnish

Cut each chicken joint in half. Melt the butter and fry the chicken pieces and the mushrooms for about 7 minutes. Remove the mushrooms. Add the milk, stock cube, water and lemon juice to the chicken and bring to the boil. Cover the pan and cook over a moderate heat for ½ hour. Remove the chicken and while it cools enough to handle make a smooth paste with 1 oz of the flour and a little water. Remove the flesh from the chicken bones and return to the liquid in the pan, stirring in the flour paste until smooth. Bring to the boil, stirring to prevent lumps and when thickened add the mushrooms. Turn into an oven-proof dish and pre-heat the oven to 220°C (Gas Mark 7). Prepare the scone topping by sifting the flour and baking powder together. Cut the margarine into small pieces and rub into the flour. Mix with sufficient water to make a soft dough. Turn on to a floured board and press lightly to the shape and size of the dish. Carefully place on top of the chicken and make crossed line patterning on the top, by dipping a knife into flour and scoring diagonally about 2 inches apart. Brush with milk and bake in the centre of the hot oven for 10 minutes or until well-risen and golden brown. Serve hot, garnished with parsley.

Sippet Pudding

Sippet is the old Cotswold name for baked 'sop' pudding — rather like today's bread and butter pudding, without the butter, as finely shredded suet was used instead. This recipe is an up-dated version of one called 'Bread Cheesecakes, in one of my old notebooks dated 1868. The retention of the brandy in the sippet itself, and served with the wine sauce, makes it a special occasion pudding — although you could use a fruit juice instead — and I have substituted milk for the 'taking of a pint of fresh cream'.

(Serves 4)
A penny loaf (about 8 ozs white bread) cut thinly
1 tablesp of brandy
2 eggs
3 ozs finely shredded suet (the vegetarian one is good)
½ teasp grated nutmeg
¾ pint milk
4 ozs sultanas or currants
2 ozs granulated sugar

Butter a pie dish and lay a slice of the bread in the bottom. Cut the rest of the bread into small triangles. Scatter about a third of the suet, fruit and sugar over the bread. Layer some of the bread pieces on top and again scatter with the suet, fruit and sugar, this time adding a little of the nutmeg. Complete with another layer of bread and use up the rest of the fruit, suet and sugar. Beat the eggs lightly. Heat the milk to just below boiling point and stir on to the eggs. Add the brandy. Mix well then pour over the bread. Leave to stand for ½ hour to allow the bread to soak up the liquid. Sprinkle the rest of the nutmeg on top. Bake at 180°C (Gas Mark 4) for 50-60 minutes in a baking tin one-third full of water. The pudding should be risen and golden and set. Sprinkle with extra sugar on the top as soon as it is cooked. Remove from the oven and keep warm to serve.

Wine Sauce for Sippet

8 fl ozs milk
2 eggs
1 tablesp caster sugar
3 fl ozs wine (white)

Warm the milk and stir in the sugar to dissolve. Whisk the eggs with the wine and add to the milk. Place the bowl over a pan of simmering water and stir until the sauce thickens. Strain through a sieve into a warmed jug to serve.

The previous Wine Sauce can be used to accompany this very old Carrot Pudding.

Carrot Pudding

Sweet vegetables, such as carrots and parsnips, were used in sweet puddings in days gone by, and their value was recognised again during World War II when housewives turned to their mothers' cook books when sugar was rationed and every vegetable in the garden was utilised. Carrot is still used in Christmas pudding for its lightness, and makes this a surprisingly delicate dish.

(Serves 4)
5 fl ozs double cream
5 fl ozs milk
1 large egg
1 large carrot, grated
1 oz white breadcrumbs
1 level tablesp sugar
1 oz butter (unsalted preferably)
a few black grapes for garnish
a few slices of glace orange or 2 ozs candied citron peel (preferably home-made)

Mix together the milk and cream and the yolk of the egg — dribble in about half of the white but no more. Add the carrot and breadcrumbs. Pour into a buttered pie dish. Melt the butter and carefully stir into the pudding mixture together with the peel or glacé fruit. Place in a pan of simmering water to reach about half way up the dish. Bake in a pre-heated oven at 170°C (Gas Mark 3) for about 45 minutes until the pudding is set in the middle. Decorate with the grapes, halved and seeded, and serve with wine sauce or thin cream.

Golden Potato Pie

Saffron is expensive but as very little is used and the colour and special light spicy taste is unlike any other, it is worth having this herb in the kitchen — even more worthwhile if you can grow it in your garden. Again, this pudding uses a vegetable — the humble potato — for its sweetness.

(Serves 4 well)
4 ozs shortcrust pastry
8 ozs potato, mashed
¼ teasp saffron stems
4 ozs butter, unsalted and softened
3 tablesps caster sugar
3 egg yolks
2 egg whites
1 tablesps rose water

Soak the saffron stems in a tablespoonful of boiling water. Line a buttered pie dish with the pastry. Beat the softened butter into the mashed potato with the sugar, add the rose water. Lightly whip the egg yolks and beat into the mixture. Whip the egg whites in a separate bowl until softly peaking. Brush the inside of the pastry case with a little of the whipped egg white then fold in the remainder, alternately with the dissolved saffron, until well blended but light in texture. Turn into the pastry case and bake in a pre-heated oven at 180°C (Gas Mark 4) for 45-50 minutes until the potato filling is completely set and richly golden. Cover with a dome of foil if browning too much.

Serve with a thin pouring custard sauce flavoured with orange zest, or a tablespoonful of sweet sherry.

Farm Toast

(Serves 4)
4 thick slices of bread
8 rashers of streaky bacon
2 large crisp eating apples (cored and cut into rings)
4 ozs Double Gloucester cheese

Fry the rashers until cooked, but not crisp, in their own fat. Remove and lightly brown the bread in the fat — you may have to add a little more. Place the fried bread on a warmed baking tray and place two rashers on each slice. Quickly soften the apple rings in the remaining fat and cover the bacon with them. Cut the cheese into very thin slivers and layer over the top of each slice. Roast quickly in a very hot oven until the cheese just starts to melt. Eat immediately.

Serve with a little salad and pickles for a tasty supper dish or snack.

Mumbled Rabbit

The name of this very old dish would suggest that it might have been contrived for toothless grannies and very young children; rabbit was the staple food of the cottager and Cotswold cooks found some pretty ingenious ways of making it seem different. This is one of the best ways to mumble a rabbit and it makes a delicious alternative to the European meat sauce served with pasta. This method was recorded as early as 1698, so is probably many years older than that. The economical use of the cooking pot is an echo of the times it hung from the chimney hook.

(Serves 4)
1½ lbs of prepared rabbit
3 eggs
1 small onion, finely chopped
3 ozs butter
bunch of mixed herbs

Wash the rabbit and cut from the bone, cut into small pieces and simmer in a pan of lightly salted boiling water with the herbs until the meat is tender. Some ten minutes before the rabbit is reckoned to be cooked, wash the eggs well and drop them carefully (still in their shells) into the pan. Remove after ten minutes and run under cold water. Shell the eggs and chop them finely. Remove the rabbit from the pan and discard the herbs — retain the liquor. Melt the butter in a saucepan. Chop the rabbit into the butter, add the onion and stir well to coat, place over a low heat and fold through the chopped eggs. Season to taste and keep warm to serve.

Serve with pasta cooked in the rabbit liquor.

Sod Eggs

Sod, meaning to boil, is a Biblical term and was used in the message to Moses in the first month of the Jewish year, when details of how the lambs were to be cooked were given to him. This old method of serving boiled eggs in a seasoned butter sauce makes a good snack.

(Serves 4)
4 eggs
4 ozs butter
1 level teasp dry English mustard
2 teasps white wine vinegar
3 teasps lemon juice
seasoning

Boil the eggs for 5 minutes exactly. Remove the shells and keep the eggs in a warm place. Melt the butter in a small pan very gently. Mix the vinegar, lemon juice and mustard together until smooth and stir into the melted butter, seasoning to taste. Cut the eggs into quarters and place in a warmed dish, pour the sauce over and serve with toast or crusty bread.

Cottage Bread (One Rising)

(Makes two loaves)
3 lb wholemeal flour
4 ozs rolled oats
1 tablesp lard
1 tablesp salt
½ pint boiling water
1 tablesp black treacle
1 tablesp dried yeast
½ pint warm water
1 tablesp sugar

Put the flour into a warmed bowl. Mix the oats, lard, salt, treacle together in a separate bowl with the boiling water and leave to cool. Mix together in a jug, the yeast and sugar with the warm water and leave until frothy. Add the oat mixture to the flour, then the yeast mix, adding more warm water if necessary to make an elastic dough, but not sticky. Knead for exactly 125 times. Divide into loaves and half-fill well greased loaf tins. Cover with oiled or greased polythene, or a clean cloth, and leave in a warm place until doubled in size. Bake in a pre-heated oven at 205°C (Gas Mark 6) for 40-45 minutes. Tap the bottom of the loaf to test if it is done — it should sound hollow. Cool on wire tray. (This bread freezes well).

Twelfth Night Cake

8 ozs self-raising flour
8 ozs sultanas
1 egg (lightly beaten)
1 teasp bicarbonate of soda
pinch of ground black pepper
4 ozs brown sugar (soft)
4 ozs butter
1 cup stout (dark)
1 teasp ground ginger
1 dried bean and 1 dried pea

Put butter, sugar, fruit and stout into a pan and bring slowly to boiling point then lower the heat and simmer for 2 minutes. Leave to cool. Sieve the dry ingredients into a mixing bowl, add the fruit mixture then the egg. Mix thoroughly and turn into a round 10-inch greased and lined tin. Cook in a pre-heated oven at 175°C (Gas Mark 4) for about 40 minutes until a skewer inserted in the centre comes out clean. When cold, decorate with glace icing, nuts and cherries.

Feggy 'obs

Feggy is the dialect term for figs — but figs in turn meant stone raisins. If you can get them, and there are a few health food shops who sell them now, these raisins are worth the trouble of stoning yourself for the taste. This recipe is quite simple and produces a kind of pastry biscuit. You can use figs instead of raisins, of course.

8 ozs shortcrust pastry
6 ozs stoned raisins (or figs)
1 egg (lightly beaten)
1 oz butter (softened)
1 tablesp demerara sugar

Roll the pastry out on a floured board into a rectangle, about ¼ inch thick. Spread with butter then sprinkle the fruit over, cover with the sugar and drizzle most of the egg over the top. Dampen the long edges and the far edge with water and roll up like a Swiss roll, sealing the edge firmly. Place the roll, join underneath, on a greased baking sheet and mark into slices with a sharp incision but do not cut through the roll at this stage. Brush with the rest of the egg and bake in a moderate oven 180°C (Gas Mark 4) for about 40 minutes until golden and cooked through. Remove from the oven and while still warm cut through the slices. Lay them flat on the baking tray and leave to cool.

Wassail Bowl

(Serves 8)
2 pints brown ale
½ pint dry sherry or dry white wine
4 small red apples
4 tablesps brown sugar
2 cinnamon sticks
½ nutmeg — grated
a shake of ground ginger
strip of lemon peel

Wash and core the apples. Place on a baking dish and fill the centres with brown sugar, pour a little of the ale in the dish and bake in a moderate oven until tender, but still whole. Heat all the other ingredients in a large pan but do not let boil. Stir to make sure that the sugar is dissolved. Heat for at least 15 minutes. Pour into a warmed bowl and place the baked apples on top. Serve immediately.

Mead

An alcoholic drink from fermented honey was being made in Britain at least 3,000 years ago, making it the oldest drink known to us in recognisable form. The Saxons reserved it for their warriors and it became a nobleman's drink: in later centuries spices were added and it became known as metheglin, but this old recipe is in its simplest form and must be very close to the original — especially if you use plain Cotswold honey and avoid strongly flavoured flower or imported types.

(Makes about 8 pints)
3 lbs plain Cotswold honey
8 pints water (soft if possible)
2ozs root ginger
2 lemons
1 oz mead yeast (baker's will do, but try to get the mead yeast)

Bruise the ginger to release the pungency by tying in a piece of muslin and hitting hard with a hammer. Add the rind of the lemon to the muslin and tie securely. Put in a large pan with the water and the juice from the lemons. Bring to the boil and allow to cool to 50°C (122°F). Stand the honey in a warm place to reach the same temperature, add to the water and stir well. Leave to reduce heat to 21°C (70°F) then remove the bag of ginger. Crumble the yeast and add to the pan. Pour into a fermentation jar, filling it about three quarters full and fit the airlock. Rest until the wine separates from the sediment (the lees), rack as necessary by siphoning to another bottle until quite clear and all gas has gone, then leave for two weeks before bottling and storing. Mead is ready to drink in six months, but improves in flavour and quality if left for a couple of years.

Pitchfork Chutney

2 lbs cooking apples
2 cloves
8 ozs sultanas
¾ pint white wine vinegar
1 large orange
4 ozs chopped nuts (walnuts for choice)
1 lb soft brown sugar
1 lemon

Grate the rinds of the orange and lemon and extract the juice. Peel and finely chop the apples. Put all ingredients in a large pan and bring to the boil. Reduce the heat and simmer for about an hour, by which time the chutney should be thick with no loose vinegar. Pot and cover while warm.

February

Remembering the Saints and the Shriven — with Love Fruit and Pancakes

February is usually looked on as a dreary month. But there is always some old tradition or feast day that the cook can turn to for inspiration.

If Candlemas Day be fair and bright,
Winter will take another flight.
If Candlemas Day be cloud and rain,
Winter is gone and will not come again

Candlemas Day, the second day of February, was once an important date in the country calendar. And, like St Swithin's Day, was observed for the portent of the coming weather. Still called St Bride's Day in remote parts of the country (a corruption of the name Bridget) it was one of many pagan traditions to be adopted by the Christian church, and in this case, it was the Celtic goddess of youth and fertility who was honoured. Later, it was the Virgin Mary who became the focus of the celebrations, and it was customary to have lighted candles in every window of the houses that could afford them, as well as a Mass with candles in pre-Reformation church services — whence the day got its latest name. Snowdrops, as symbolic of purity, are still referred to by older country folk as Candlemas bells.

St Valentine's Day, on the 14th, is still a red-letter day, although the origin may not be celebrated. Love messages come today in cards and flowers, so in keeping with the romanticism I have included recipes using the first food symbolic of love, the apple.

Valentine was a Bishop of Rome, martyred on the eve of the great festival of Lupercalia when young Romans won their sweethearts by lottery. 'Scratch Gloucestershire and find Rome' is a well-worn phrase, so it can be safely reckoned that the Roman legions who tramped their way across the Cotswolds, as well as the settled Roman communities, celebrated with feasting and courtship. St Valentine therefore became the patron saint of lovers.

In direct contrast to the feasting and fun of St Valentine's Day, is the advent of Lent. Using up the foods and meats forbidden during the Lenten fasting, the housewives created the pancake — a humble concoction of flour and eggs — before the repentant were shriven of their sins. Shrove Tuesday is celebrated throughout the kingdom with pancakes and in living memory, the bell which called the faithful to church on that day became known as the Pancake Bell — a single bell tolled was interpreted as 'Pan On, Pan On', and became a signal to start making the batter ready for mid-day dinner. Gloucestershire pancakes are not really a batter pancake, more like a scone, while Tewkesbury Batters are traditional batter, baked, but in saucers! Well, all this variation is what makes regional cookery so fascinating.

Pancake Tuesday's a happy day
If we don't have a holiday, we'll all run away,
Where shall we run to? Up High Lane,
But here comes the teacher with a great big cane.

This school rhyme dates back to the days when Shrove Tuesday was a public holiday.

William Cobbett, the dour old Radical who included the Cotswolds in his Rural Rides, would have none of the frivolity of customary celebration and romance — in his 'Advice to Young Men' he simply stated:

Never mind about the piece of needlework,
the tambouring, the maps of the world
made by her needlework —
get to see her at work upon a mutton chop.

The workaday pancake would have probably found favour with him!

Love Apple Soup

Tomatoes were always called 'love apples' by my grandparents. And certainly, it is said, that when they came to Europe in Tudor times, they were treated with caution as they were reputed to arouse 'dangerous passions'. Wary cooks, therefore, put them in stews and soups in the hope that the cooking process would weaken the powers somewhat of the *pomme d'amour* which the French had called the tomato through an error in translation! It was not until the mid-Victorian age that the tomato was adopted into the British diet, both as an ingredient in cooking and raw in salads.

(Serves 4)
1 lb tomatoes, skinned and roughly chopped
6 ozs carrots, prepared and finely chopped
1 large (or 2 small) eating apples, prepared and chopped
½ oz butter
2 teasps vegetable oil
1 onion peeled and finely chopped
3 bay leaves and a bouquet garni of thyme and marjoram
2 pints good vegetable stock
2 cloves garlic, peeled and finely chopped
4 tablesps double cream and croutons for garnish

Melt the butter and oil together and cook the onion and garlic over a low heat for about 15 minutes until the onion is soft and transparent. Add the carrot and stir until all the fat has been absorbed, then add the rest of the ingredients (excluding the cream and croutons). Bring to the boil, then cover with a lid and simmer for 45 minutes. Discard the herbs and pass the soup through a sieve — or liquidise — until smooth. Season to taste and return to a clean pan to heat through; do not allow to boil. Serve with a swirl of cream and croutons. Chopped chives or a sprig of parsley are also good garnishes if you have no croutons.

Cheese and Vegetable Paté

(Serves 6)
1 small onion, finely chopped
1 stick celery
4 ozs button mushrooms
8 ozs curd cheese
4 ozs cream cheese
1 tablesp creamed horseradish
3 tablesps chopped parsley
2 tablesps chopped chives
seasoning to taste
1 clove garlic, crushed with salt
1 oz margarine
parsley for garnish

Melt the margarine and gently soften the onion and garlic for about 5 minutes. Chop the celery and mushrooms very fine. Put into a mixing bowl and add the fried onion and the remaining ingredients. Check for seasoning, then beat well together. Spoon into individual pots, cover with cling film (as the smell of the garlic might spread to other foods in the fridge), and chill. Serve, garnished with tiny sprigs of parsley, with crisp toast fingers.

Collops

The austerity of Lent was well prepared for by our ancestors. The Monday before the start of Lent on Ash Wednesday became known as 'Collop Monday', because this was the last opportunity for eating meat, which was forbidden during the Lenten fast. This simple dish is still good enough, if using best fillet steak, although other meats, such as pork or lamb could be used, to serve to guests. 'Collops' mean slices of meat.

(Serves 4)
1 lb fillet steak
1 dessertsp flour
1½ ozs butter
½ small onion, finely grated
1 clove garlic (optional)
¼ pint good brown stock
2 tablesps claret (or good red wine)
seasoning

Slice the meat thinly. Season the flour and put into a plastic bag, add the meat slices and coat well. Heat the butter in a frying pan and fry the onion and crushed garlic for about 7 minutes. Tip in any residue of seasoned flour and blend in. Add the collops and braise for 5 minutes, turning once. Add the stock and wine and simmer gently for 15 minutes. Season to taste. Serve immediately with creamed potatoes and green vegetables.

Pickled Grapes

1 lb grapes (green are best)
½ pint water
1 teasp mixed pickling spice
¼ pint white vinegar
4 ozs white sugar

Wash the grapes and remove all stalks. Pack into jars. Boil the rest of the ingredients together for 15 minutes. Strain and cool. Pour over the grapes to cover. Seal and store for at least 3 weeks before using. Good accompaniment to meat and poultry dishes.

Spiced Peaches

Large tin of peach halves
12 whole cloves
3 tablesps brown sugar
1 oz butter
Pinch each of cinnamon and ground nutmeg

Drain the peaches. Stud with the cloves. Place, cut side uppermost, in a lightly buttered dish inside a grill pan. Mix the sugar and spices together and sprinkle over the peaches. Dot with butter. Grill for 4-5 minutes. Serve cold with cut meats, or hot with ice-cream, as a dessert.

Gloucestershire Pancakes

The tradition of eating pancakes on Shrove Tuesday, the day when the faithful were 'shriven', or absolved from their sins, before the rigours of Lent, arose from using up the forbidden foods such as eggs and dairy produce for the forty days. This old-time recipe for the traditional pancake which evolved in the county is quite unusual in having suet as an ingredient and frying in lard. This combination gives a distinctive quality to the pancakes, which, again unusually, derive from a dough-like mixture, rather than the more nationally known batter. This makes Gloucestershire pancakes ideal for a base on which to put a slice of meat or tomatoes and cheese for a more substantial main course dish.

(Serves 4)
6 ozs plain flour
1 egg, beaten
3 ozs good shredded suet
1 teasp baking powder
a pinch of salt
a little milk for mixing
1 oz lard for frying

Mix the flour, salt and baking powder together with the suet into a bowl. Blend in the egg and enough milk to make a firm dough. Roll out lightly on to a floured board and cut into 2-inch rounds. Fry in the melted hot lard until golden brown each side. Serve hot topped with meat or cheese, accompanied by a salad.

Green Cream Fish Dish

(Serves 4)
1 lb white fish
½ cucumber
1 tablesp vinegar, white wine preferably
8 fl ozs mayonnaise
small lettuce
1 tablesp fresh parsley, finely chopped
1 lemon
1 tablesp chives, finely snipped
8 ozs prepared prawns
1 small onion, finely chopped

Put one pint of water, the vinegar and two slices of the lemon in a saucepan. Bring to the boil. Add the cleaned white fish. Bring back to boiling point, reduce heat and simmer for 1 minute. Remove from the heat, cover with a lid and let get cold. Mix the mayonnaise, onion, parsley and chives together. Season to taste. Line a flat dish with washed and dried lettuce leaves. Flake the cold fish and lay on top, arranging the prawns attractively on top. Spoon the cream dressing, which should have turned a pale green, over the fish and garnish with the rest of the lemon, and slices of cucumber.

Sweetheart Fillet

(Serves 4)
1 lb pork fillet
4 ozs dried apricots
½ oz arrowroot
½ pint stock
1 fl oz orange juice
creamed potatoes and broccoli spears

Pre-heat the oven to 200°C (Gas Mark 6). Cut the fillet in half lengthwise. Keep back 4 apricots for the sauce and place the rest down the centre of one half of the pork fillet. Season lightly and place the other half on top. Tie together at regular intervals with fine string. Place in a roasting tin and cover first with the orange juice, then the stock. Cover and cook for about 1¼ hours. If the juices run clear when tested with a skewer, it is done. Remove from the pan and keep warm.

Mix the arrowroot with a spoonful of water in a small saucepan and strain in the juices from the roasting pan. Bring to the boil, stirring all the time, then simmer for a further 5 minutes. Cut the apricots into small pieces and add to the sauce. Tip into a liquidiser or blender and process until quite smooth. To serve, slice the fillet thinly and arrange 3 slices on each warmed plate into a heart shape. Pipe creamed potatoes around the fillet to define the heart shape more boldly. Spoon the sauce carefully over the fillet — this will give an attractive glazed appearance. Then place well-drained broccoli spears across the potato edge to represent an arrow piercing the heart.

Eve's Pudding

If you wish a good pudding, pray
mind what you take.
Two pennyworth of eggs when
they're twelve for a groat.
Take of the same fruit which Eve
once did cozen,
Well pound and well chopped, at
least half a dozen.
Six ounces of bread (let your maid
eat the crust),
The crumb must be grated as fine
as dust.
Six ounces of currants, but pray
wash them clean,
Lest they grate in your mouth, you
know what I mean.
Six ounces of sugar will not make
it too sweet.
Some salt and some nutmeg, to
make it complete.
To this you may add, if you're
willing and handy,
Some good lemon peel and a large
glass of brandy.
Three hours let it boil, without
hurry or fluster
Then serve it quite hot, with good
melted butter.

Although this is very good — and does not need three hours boiling — the equally old-time Adam and Eve Pudding is a much more attractive pudding, and you can taste the 'love fruit' more distinctly.

Adam and Eve Pudding

(Serves 6)
1 lb cooking apples
6 ozs caster sugar
1 tablesp lemon juice
4 ozs butter
2 eggs
1 teasp grated lemon rind
4 ozs self-raising flour
pinch of salt

Pre-heat the oven to 180°C (Gas Mark 4). Butter a deep pie dish. Peel and core the apples and slice into the dish. Sprinkle each layer with the lemon juice and half the sugar. Cream together the butter and rest of the sugar, add the eggs and the flour alternately and beat until light and fluffy, adding the lemon rind last. Spoon the mixture over the apples. Stand the dish on a baking sheet and bake for about 1½ hours until the sponge is risen and golden brown. Serve, dredged with icing sugar, if liked, and whipped cream to which a tablespoonful of sherry, a pinch of ginger, or rosewater has been added.

Pan on Pancakes — Traditional Plain Pancakes

(Serves 4)
4 ozs plain flour
½ pint milk and water mixed
1 egg
lard (or oil) for frying
pinch of salt
To serve:
2 tablesps caster sugar, and 1 lemon

Sift the flour and salt together into a mixing bowl. Make a well in the centre, add the egg then the milk gradually, beating well until bubbles break the surface. Leave for at least half an hour, then beat again to check for consistency. The batter should be at pouring thickness. Heat enough lard or oil to cover the base of a heavy frying pan. Increase heat. Pour in enough batter to thinly cover the base. Tip the pan to even out the batter. Cook for a few minutes until the edges start to curl. Flip over with a fish slice (or toss over if you feel confident!) and cook the other side. Keep warm on a plate over a pan of simmering water until all are cooked. Serve by squeezing lemon juice over the surface, sprinkle with the sugar, then roll up.

Tewkesbury Saucer Batters

Saucers were originally shallow dishes for sauces — hence their name — then became dishes for cooking small pies and puddings before they held teacups. Tewkesbury Saucer Batters are traditionally filled with soft or stewed fruits sandwiched between two baked batters. This is a very old recipe and quite delicious if raspberries or strawberries are used for the filling.

(Serves 2 — large helpings)
4 ozs plain flour
Pinch of salt
1 egg, separated
½ pint milk
Filling:
8 ozs soft fruit
2 ozs granulated sugar

Soften the fruit first, by placing in an ovenproof dish sprinkling the sugar over, then covering with a lid and leaving until the juices run. Sieve the flour and salt into a basin, beat in the yolk of the egg and the milk, then whip it vigorously for a few minutes. Leave to stand for ½ hour. Pre-heat the oven to 230°C (Gas Mark 8). Whip the egg white until stiff and standing in peaks. Fold into the batter lightly, then immediately pour it into well-buttered deep oven-proof saucers, or dishes which are about 6-inch in diameter and saucer-shaped. You need 4 for 2 puddings. Divide the batter between the saucers and place in the oven on baking sheets, together with the covered dish of fruit. Cook for about 15-20 minutes, until the batter is golden and the edges are coming away from the saucers. Remove from the oven and ease two batters onto serving dishes, hollow side up. Fill with the hot fruit, then cover with the batter from the other two saucers, hollow side down, sandwiching the fruit. Dust with sugar and serve hot.

Sausage and Onion Popovers

The same batter mix can be used to make this tasty savoury supper dish. In this case the individual baking saucers should, ideally, be 'larded' with dripping to give them their distinctive taste.

(Serves 4)
5 ozs plain flour
2 eggs
1 pint milk
12 ozs sausage meat
1 large cooking apple
2 onions, skinned and peeled and cored thinly sliced
dripping (or lard) for greasing
1 teasp finely chopped fresh parsley
½ oz butter
seasoning

Pre-heat the oven to 220°C (Gas Mark 7). Make the batter as described in previous recipe. Break the sausage meat down with a fork in a mixing bowl, grate the apple into it, add seasoning and the parsley. Mix all together and form into 16 small balls. Heat four pint sized dishes, which have been generously greased with dripping (or lard) until the fat sizzles. Place 4 sausage balls into each dish and cook in the oven for 10-12 minutes, turning once. Pour the batter over the sausage balls and return to the oven for a further 35-40 minutes until the batter is well risen and golden brown.

While the batters are cooking, make the onion sauce by cooking the onion in the remaining milk, until soft. Melt the butter in a pan and stir in the remaining 1 oz of flour, cooking over a low heat for 1 minute to blend. Gradually stir in the onion and milk, then bring to the boil and simmer until thickened. Season to taste. To serve, pour a little of the onion sauce in the hollow of the batters as soon as they are cooked and eat immediately.

Chocolate Truffles

(Makes about 36)
4 ozs plain chocolate
2 egg yolks
3 heaped tablesps sieved icing sugar
2 ozs butter

Break the chocolate into small pieces and melt slowly in a basin over a pan of hot water. Beat together the butter and sugar then beat in the egg yolks. Stir in the melted chocolate. Leave to firm up a little before rolling into small balls. Toss in cocoa powder, chocolate vermicelli or fine coconut, and place in small paper cases to set. These make very pretty and tasty gifts.

Valentine Plum Buns

Plums in this case mean currants. These traditional buns seem to have been lost to this area, but were originally shaped in the form of weavers' shuttles and were popular in the cloth-weaving valleys of the west Cotswolds.

1 lb plain flour
½ oz fresh (or ½ tablesp dried yeast
2 ozs butter
4 fl ozs warm milk
8 ozs currants
1 egg
1 dessertsp sugar
pinch of salt
2 fl ozs warm water

Cream the yeast and sugar together, mix in the warm water and leave for 20 minutes, when it should be quite frothy. Sift the flour and salt together in a warmed bowl. Melt the butter in a pan, add the milk and beat in the egg. Add the yeast mixture and the milk mixture to the flour, then stir in the currants. Mix to a smooth dough and knead for 3-4 minutes. Cover with a cloth and leave in a warm place to rise. This should take about ½ hour and the dough should be doubled in size. Knead again, then divide into 10 equally sized pieces. Shape each into a shuttle — a kind of long oval — and place on greased baking sheets. Wring a clean cloth out in warm water until it is just damp. Cover the buns with this, then leave for another ½ hour in a warm place to prove. Brush with beaten egg and bake in a pre-heated oven 200°C (Gas Mark 6) for 25-30 minutes. Cool on a wire tray. Serve, split and buttered.

Candlemas Cake

This potato cake was probably introduced by the Irish, and was popular in the celebration of Candlemas, the feast of the Purification of St Mary the Virgin. The Celts held a feast at Candlemas because it was the start of the lambing season and it is therefore fitting that the sheeplands of the Cotswolds should have taken this custom as their own.

(Makes 8 small or 6 medium cakes)
8 ozs cooked potatoes, mashed
8 ozs plain flour
½ teasp bicarbonate of soda
2 ozs mature cheese, grated
2 fl ozs buttermilk
2 ozs dripping
1 tablesp fresh parsley finely chopped
seasoning

Pre-heat the oven to 200°C (Gas Mark 6). Melt the dripping and stir in the flour and bicarbonate of soda. Then add the potato and cheese. Stir in the parsley and light seasoning, adding enough of the buttermilk to mix to a fairly soft dough. Roll out on a floured board to about ½ inch thickness, then cut into rounds with a 3-inch cutter. Bake on a greased sheet for 15-20 minutes until risen and golden brown. Serve warm, split and buttered.

Initial Biscuits

Cotswold maids have stopped the custom of throwing an apple peel over their shoulder to see what initial it formed as it fell, foretelling who their sweetheart would be. These little biscuits, shaped in the initials of your guests, or just the family members, make a personal addition to the table and are good accompaniments to syllabub or ice-cream, or simply with a cup of tea or coffee.

(Makes 16)
5 ozs butter
10 ozs self-raising flour
grated rind of ½ lemon
5 ozs caster sugar
1 egg, lightly beaten
2 ozs ground almonds

Pre-heat the oven to 180°C (Gas Mark 4). Beat the butter and sugar together until fluffy. Beat in half the egg, stir in the flour, almonds and lemon rind, then the rest of the egg. Roll small pieces of the soft dough between lightly floured hands and shape into initials. Place on a well-buttered baking tray and cook for about 10 minutes. The biscuits should be honey-gold coloured, not brown, but allow to get quite cool before removing from the tray with a palette knife to harden off.

Family Fun Punch (Non-Alcoholic)

2 pints apple juice
2 limes
1 stick cinnamon
1 pint water
4 tablesps brown sugar
10 cloves

Cut 4 thin slices from one of the limes and reserve for decoration. Use the juice from the remainder and that of the second lime, and add to the rest of the ingredients in a large pan. Simmer gently for about 10 minutes, taste for sweetness and spiciness, adding to personal likes. Turn into a punch bowl and float the lime slices on top.

March

Wild, Mild and Mothering

March, hack ham
If it comes in like a lion
It goes out like a lamb
As wild as a March hare.. .
Daffodils that come before the swallow dares
And take the winds of March with beauty…

March, the first month of the Roman year, was named after the god, Mars; the farming Anglo-Saxons called it Hiyd Monath, 'Stormy month', and poets from Chaucer to Shakespeare to Browning penned something on its wild or mild ways.

The wildness of a March hare is tamed when jugged — especially if it is marinated first to break down the tough fibres usually associated with wild game. Hares have been part of the countryman's diet for nearly 3,000 years, and an Act of Parliament in 1723 was passed to curb poaching the hare for fear it would be wiped out in the British countryside forever. For those who find hare too strong (for it is certainly game with all its characteristics), I have given a very old recipe for Cotswold rabbit. Rabbits were introduced to Britain by the Romans who established colonies of the 'coneys' as a kind of wild larder wherever they settled. Certainly, in the Middle Ages, rabbit was highly esteemed by both nobleman and peasant.

This is the season for spring lamb. The ancient breed of Cotswold sheep, with their distinctive mane-like fleece, have always been known as the Cotswold Lions. Today, they are a protected rare breed but there is plenty of home-grown lamb still on the hills and wolds, and the delicate meat of spring lamb deserves careful cooking to bring out the special subtle flavour.

I'll to thee a simnel bring
'Gainst thou go a-mothering.
So that when she blesses thee,
half that blessing you'll give me.

Herrick captures the origin of Mothering Sunday in this verse, and in the Middle Ages it was the 'mother church' of the parish which was visited by the smaller church congregations. In Elizabethan times the 'mother' became associated with parentage, and that probably arose through confusing the date with Lady Day, on March 25 which celebrates the Mother of God. However, the mother of the family quite rightly became part of the focus of the day. Mothering Sunday, with its long history, was a quite different custom from the now commercialised Mother's Day, which evolved as a campaign to honour the status of motherhood in America where the Senate passed the motion to have a public holiday to mark Mother's Day in 1913, and manufacturers this side of the Atlantic confused the two in the 50s to exploit a market which has increased ever since.

Mothering Sunday, falling on the fourth Sunday in Lent, was the day on which bound apprentices and servant girls were allowed home to visit their mothers. Traditionally, they gathered posies of primroses and violets from the hedgerows as they made their long walk home, and the girls took their mother a simnel cake as proof of the culinary skills learnt 'in service'. Simnel cake is now more often associated with Easter, but in the Cotswolds it was always a part of the Mothering Sunday fare. Despite it being mid-Lent, the family gathering sat down to a feast of roast lamb, with suet or rice pudding, or custard, but the centrepiece and often the only dish in poorer households — was the dish of frumenty. The Stroud valleys folk called it fermitty, and it was often taken round to friends as well. This was mother's treat for her children on her special day.

Simnel takes its name from the Latin word simila, which indicates that "the very best wheat flour" was used for this important cake. The eleven almond paste balls edging the rich fruit cake symbolize Christ's disciples; Judas, the faithless one is omitted.

March in the Cotswolds calendar is highlighted by the prestigious National Hunt Festival at Cheltenham, which includes the coveted Gold Cup. The Queen Mother always attended, making her customary stop at the thatched bakery at Prestbury to receive a special gift of chocolates — and so another much celebrated mother had her personal tradition established in the Cotswolds.

Prestbury Loaf

It seems appropriate to begin this month's collection of recipes by paying tribute to the village which was the birthplace of the legendary jockey, Fred Archer, and is now so famous for staging the Cheltenham Races. But this is not a bread loaf — on which we could imagine the great little jockey 'supped of toast' or even produced at the thatched bakery in the village street. It is a meat loaf, rather like a paté, and as such makes an excellent starter served with toast fingers and garnished with parsley.

(Serves 10)
12 ozs pig's liver
1 lb pork sausagemeat
1 lb lean minced beef
1 small onion
5 tablesps cider
1 teasp dried mixed herbs
1 teasp salt
1 teasp black pepper

Mince the liver and onion and mix together with all the ingredients until well-blended and smooth. Spoon into a 21b size loaf tin and press down firmly. Stand the tin in a roasting tin containing about one inch depth of water. Bake in a preheated oven at 180°C (Gas Mark 5) for 1½hours. Cool in the tin before turning out. (This meat loaf also freezes well.)

Queen Of Soups

(Serves 8)
1 lb potatoes, peeled and sliced
1 lb leeks, washed and sliced
2 medium onions, peeled and sliced
2 pints chicken stock
2 tablesps lemon juice
2 ozs butter
7 oz single cream (or tin of evaporated milk)

Melt the butter in a large pan and fry the prepared vegetables gently for about 3 minutes to soften. Add the stock, season to taste. Bring to the boil, reduce heat and cover the pan, simmer 45 minutes until the vegetables are thoroughly cooked. Sieve or liquidise until smooth. Return to the pan, add the cream or evaporated milk and the lemon juice, stirring to prevent curdling. Reheat but do not boil. Serve with croutons or sprigs of parsley.

Mrs Garne's Salad Dressing

1 yolk of egg
½ teasp of made mustard
seasoning and sugar to taste

Mix ½ pint of salad oil in slowly (with the rest of the ingredients) until it become quite stiff, then add a little tarragon vinegar, some common vinegar and a drop of Worcester sauce, and cream to taste.

Jugged Hare

(Serves 4-6)
1 hare, jointed
2 tablesps oil
½ pint good stock
2 medium onions, or 6 small shallots
2 sticks celery
about 6 fl ozs wine vinegar
2 tablesps redcurrant jelly
2 cloves garlic
4 ozs mushrooms
2 carrots
1 wineglass port
1 lemon
2 bay leaves
pinch of mace
small bunch of parsley, chopped
pinch of powdered cloves
freshly ground black pepper

Wash the hare joints and marinate in enough wine vinegar to cover them. Cover and leave overnight in a cool place. Drain well and pat dry. Heat the oil and brown the joints. Put into an ovenproof casserole and cook the sliced vegetables in the oil left in the pan. Add to the casserole together with the herbs, stock, seasoning and a strip of rind from the lemon and the juice from the whole lemon. Cook in a covered dish in a moderate oven — 180 °C (Gas Mark 4) for 2 hours. Reduce the heat another mark down to low, and cook for a further 1½ - 2 hours until the hare is really tender when pierced with a skewer, but the meat should not be falling off the bones. Remove the joints to a warmed serving dish. Reduce the liquid quickly in a small pan, add the port and redcurrant jelly, stirring to blend smoothly and serve with jacket potatoes and extra redcurrant jelly.

Cotswold Rabbit

(Serves 4)
1 rabbit, jointed
2 large onions, roughly chopped
2 rashers streaky bacon, diced
1 oz butter
2 tablesps oil
2 tablesps Dijon mustard
6 fl ozs dry white wine
pinch thyme
seasoning to taste

Preheat the oven to 240°C (Gas Mark 9). Heat the butter and oil together in a frying pan (the oil stops the butter from browning and burning) and gently fry the bacon pieces until the fat runs, transfer to a casserole dish. Next fry the rabbit joints until lightly browned, add to the dish, then soften the onion in the remaining fat. Add to the casserole, sprinkling with the thyme and seasoning. Stir the mustard with the wine to blend and bring to just below boiling point. Pour over the ingredients in the casserole dish. Reduce the heat to 190°C (Gas Mark 5) and cook in a closely covered dish for 1½-2 hours until the rabbit is tender. Serve with plain boiled, or mashed potatoes and carrots.

Rack of Lamb with Herbs

About 3 lb joint of best end of neck of lamb — get the butcher to chine the meat and saw a line across the cutlet bones about halfway down. Remove the chine bone and boil to make good stock gravy to serve with the lamb.

2 tablesps each of fresh rosemary, parsley and chives, chopped
1 tablesp corn oil
seasoning
Garnish:
sprigs of parsley and rosemary
1 lemon or lime

Remove any loose bones and trim the top edge of the cutlets to leave a couple of inches of bare bone at the top. Preheat the oven to 190°C (Gas Mark 5). Make slits in the joint just above the sawn edge of the bones in sufficient number for the exposed bone ends to be pushed through. Lay the joint, skin side down, on a working surface and sprinkle evenly with the chopped herbs. Roll the meat firmly round the herbs to make a roll, pushing the end bones through the slits to secure. Tie between each bone with fine string. Season the fat side, then place in a roasting tin. Brush over with the oil and cover the exposed bone ends with foil to prevent burning. Cook for 1½ hours until the juices run clear when the meat is pierced. Remove from the tin and let the joint rest for 15 minutes before garnishing with the fresh herbs and cutlet frills (if desired) on the bone ends to serve. Cut into thick slices, removing the string ties, and serve with vegetables and wedges of the lemon or lime.

Honeyed Lamb In Cider

Leg of lamb
1 bottle dry cider
2 tablesps rosemary
1 level teasp ground ginger
1 rounded tablesp thick honey
seasoning

Preheat the oven to 190°C (Gas Mark 5). Wipe the lamb thoroughly, then rub all over with the seasoning and ginger. Place in a deep pan. Spread the honey over the joint, rubbing it well in with the back of the spoon. Pour in the cider to come about 2 inches up the side of the lamb. Roast for about 2 hours basting frequently. Test with a skewer to see if done — the juices should run clear. Transfer to a warmed serving dish and rest for at least 15 minutes before carving. Reduce the liquid from the pan by boiling rapidly, serve with the lamb.

Cheltenham Pudding

(Serves 6)
6 ozs plain flour
6 ozs shredded suet
4 ozs sugar
3 ozs fresh white breadcrumbs
2 ozs raisins
2 ozs currants
1 small lemon
2 eggs
¼ pint milk
1 teasp baking powder
½ teasp grated nutmeg
pinch of salt

Mix all the dry ingredients together in a bowl. Add the grated rind of the lemon. Beat the eggs and milk together lightly and add, with the juice of the lemon. Mix well together. Spoon into a well buttered pie dish and bake in a moderate oven, preheated to 190°C (Gas Mark 5) for 1½ hours until risen and nicely brown. Serve with thin pouring custard.

Queen Pudding

This is the recipe in one of my old notebooks, dated 1886, and is what is now generally called 'Queen of Puddings'. I give it exactly as written.

(Serves 4)
½ lb breadcrumbs
1 pint new milk
2 ozs butter
the yolk of 4 eggs
sugar to taste and a little lemon flavouring

Boil the breadcrumbs and milk together, then add the sugar, butter and eggs. When these are well mixed take a tart dish and bake it in it until a light brown. Now put a layer of jam on the top of this, then the whites of the eggs, beaten to a stiff froth with a little sifted sugar. Smooth it over with a knife dipped in boiling water and bake for 10 minutes in a slow oven.

Valley Fermitty

(Serves 4)
4 heaped tablesps cracked wheat
2 oranges or lemons
2 tablesps caster sugar
5 ozs double cream

Put the wheat in sufficient cold water to cover completely and leave to soak overnight. Strain, and cover again with 2 pints fresh water. Leave to soak again for a whole day. Stir and strain the liquid into a saucepan (keep the wheat for stuffing or give it to the garden birds). Add the strained juice from the fruit, reserve the skins. Add the sugar and bring to the boil. Keep at a low rolling boil for about 10 minutes, stirring all the time, until thickened. Cool then add the cream. Pour into a dish to set and grate the rind on top. This is really delicious if a tablespoon each of honey and whisky are mixed together and drizzled over the top, with a dollop of whipped cream afloat, at the point of serving.

The next two recipes are taken from an early 15th century receipt book, although the ingredients are recognisable even in their original spelling; there is no indication of quantities, but I include them here for their historic value.

Eggs En Poche (1430)

Take egge, breke him and boyle him in hot water. Then take him up as whole as thou may. Then take floure and mix with mylke and cast thereto sugre or honey and a little gynger. Colour it with saffron. Lay thine egge in a dishe and pour on ye sauce. Sprinkle with allspice.

Omlette (1430)

Take and drawe the whyte and the yolkes of eggs through a straynor. Take onyons and shred them small. Then take fair butter or greece, and fry the onyons therin. Then caste the egge in the panne and break the onyons together and let them fry together a littul while. Then take them up and serve on a fayre disshe.

My next recipe is a baked herb version.

Baked Herb Omelette

8 small or 6 medium sized eggs
2 leeks, washed and sliced
4 spring onions, chopped
4 ozs spinach, washed and chopped
3 tablesps chopped parsley
seasoning
1 tablesp walnuts, chopped
3 tablesps chopped herbs — tarragon, chives, chervil, coriander or dill or a mixture

Reheat the oven to 180°C (Gas Mark 4). Beat the eggs in a large bowl until frothy then add all other ingredients. Mix well and season to taste. Pour into a well-buttered dish. Cover with foil and bake for 30 minutes. Uncover and cook for a further 15-20 minutes until the top is nicely browned. Serve hot or cold with tomato, onion and orange salad.

Stuffed Beer Pancakes

(Serves 4)
4 ozs plain flour
4 fl ozs milk
4 fl ozs beer
4 eggs
3 ozs butter
8 ozs cream cheese
1 small onion, chopped fine
1 clove garlic, crushed
8 ozs button mushrooms
seasoning
1 tablesp chopped basi1, or a mix of parsley and chives
4 tablesps grated parmesan or tasty hard cheese
5 fl ozs single cream

Beat together the flour, 2 of the eggs, the beer and milk. Melt 2 ozs of the butter and add — beat well until bubbles form on the surface. Cover and leave to stand for an hour. Melt the rest of the butter in a pan and sweat the onion and garlic together for about 5 minutes. Add the prepared and chopped mushrooms and fry gently for 2 minutes. Leave aside to cool, then mix in the remaining ingredients except the hard cheese and cream. Leave to get cold while making the pancakes. Reheat the oven to 180°C (Gas Mark 4). Melt a small knob of butter in a frying pan, then fry about 2 tablesps of the batter at a time for about 2 minutes each side. Keep each pancake warm on a clean cloth until all are cooked. Fill each pancake with the mushroom and cream cheese mixture and roll up. Place side by side in an ovenproof dish. Scatter with the hard cheese and pour the cream over. Bake for 20-25 minutes. Serve hot.

Simnel Cake

6 ozs butter or margarine
6 ozs caster sugar
3 eggs
3 tablesps milk
6 ozs self-raising flour
2 ozs plain flour
pinch of salt
pinch of mixed spice
2 ozs mixed peel
6 ozs sultanas
4 ozs raisins
4 ozs currants
the white of 1 egg
12 ozs almond paste (marzipan)

Preheat the oven to 160°C (Gas Mark 3). Divide the almond paste into three equal portions and keep wrapped until ready to use to prevent drying out. Cream the fat with the sugar until light and fluffy. Beat in the eggs and milk alternately with the flours, sieved together with the salt. Beat in the spice, peel and dried fruits. Place half the mixture in a well-greased and lined 7-inch cake tin. Roll out one third of the almond paste, place on top then cover with the remaining cake mixture. Smooth the top and bake for about 2 hours until a skewer inserted in the middle comes out clean. Cover the top with foil if browning too quickly. Allow to rest in the tin for about 10 minutes before turning out on a rack to cool. When completely cold, roll out the second portion of almond paste to fit the top, trimming to neaten. Press the edges down firmly to seal the paste to the cake. Divide the remaining paste into 11 equally sized balls and place evenly round the edge. Brush over with the lightly whisked egg white, and brown very lightly under the grill to give a glisten to the cake. Tie a yellow ribbon round the cake to serve.

Victoria Sponge

One of my lasting memories of my grandparents' home was the picture of a lace capped Queen Victoria hung over the small table which held the large family bible. Every night Granny Lewis made a little bow to the old lady in the heavy oak frame and bid her 'goodnight'. With a child's curiosity I questioned why Granny singled out the formidable old lady from the number of distant relatives who also looked down sombrely from the rose patterned walls. "We were taught as children that she was mother to us all," she explained, so for a long while I thought that Queen Victoria was our Gran's Mum! And I believed that it was she who had shown Gran how to make Victoria sponge.

6 ozs butter
6 ozs caster sugar
6 ozs self-raising flour
3 eggs, beaten

Preheat the oven to 190°C (Gas Mark 5). Butter and base line two 7-inch sandwich tins. Beat the butter and sugar together until very light and fluffy. Add the eggs, a little at a time, beating well between each addition. Fold in half the flour using a metal spoon, mix well but do not beat, then fold in the remainder. Spoon into the tins and bake for about 20 minutes until well risen and starting to shrink slightly from the edge of the tins. Leave to cool for about 3 minutes before turning out on a cake rack to cool completely. When cold, sandwich together with jam and dredge the top with caster or icing sugar.

A wide variety of flavours and fillings can be made to this basic recipe. If using cocoa powder for a chocolate sponge, replace 3 level tablesps of flour with the same amount of cocoa powder.

Maids of Honour

It is traditionally thought that these little tartlets were named by Henry VIII after the Maids of Honour attending Court. The recipe was a closely guarded secret for many years — and one wonders whether the original one was ever revealed for there seem many variations. The pastry base, lemon and almond flavouring seem to be common ingredients, but in some recipes the cheese is replaced by cake crumbs. I think this old recipe is probably nearer the Tudor one, as sweet curd cheese was a popular filling for small tartlets at that time.

(Makes 16)
8 ozs puff pastry
8 ozs curd or cottage cheese, sieved
3 ozs sugar
2 ozs currants
½ oz blanched almonds, chopped
grated rind of 1 lemon
1 egg, beaten
2 teasps brandy
½ oz melted butter

Preheat the oven to 190°C (Gas Mark 5). Roll out the pastry and line 16 greased patty tins. Beat together all the ingredients and half fill the tartlet cases. Bake for 25-30 minutes until risen and golden brown. Leave to cool on a wire tray.

Mrs Radway's Dandelion Wine

This recipe is signed, 'H Radway, Ampney', and in the order in which it is written in my little black notebook it must be just over 100 years old.

2 quarts of dandelion flowers
3 lbs sugar
Up to 1 gallon of water
1 orange
2 lemons
½ lb raisins
wine yeast

After measuring the flowers, lay them to dry a while then pour some boiling water over them and let them stand two days. Strain and squeeze them well. Boil the liquid with the sugar and the peel of the lemons and orange for 20 minutes. The juice of them to be added when cool enough to barm. (Leave to get lukewarm then add the yeast and recommended nutrient tablet). The peel to be taken out and the raisins to be cut open and put in when it is put into the barrel. (Modern day wine-making would allow for this to be done before putting into a fermentation jar). Fit an airlock and leave until fermentation has ceased and the wine has cleared before it is siphoned off and bottled.

Madge Craddock's Turkish Delight (1890)

Dissolve 2 ozs of leaf gelatine in 1½ breakfast cup of cold water for 20 minutes then add ¼ of a cup more water and 4 large cups of white sugar (not caster). Boil for 15 minutes. Add 2 teasps of essence of lemon, 1 teasps of vanilla essence and a pinch of tartaric acid. Wet two soup plates and pour in half the mixture in one. Colour the remainder pink, then pour into the other plate. Stand in a cool place for 24 hours. Cut into pieces and roll in icing sugar. Dip knife in sugar when cutting up.

Miss Rix's Apple Ginger (1887)

2 lbs hard apples either peeled or not, as preferred, cut each into 8 pieces. Put them in cold water as they are cut. Make a rich syrup of 3lbs lump sugar, nearly a teacup of water with 1 oz of essence of ginger. Boil the syrup well, then put the apples (drained well) into the syrup and boil until transparent. Be sure to keep the cover on all the time it is boiling and the apples in water or they will not become transparent. (About 20 minutes boiling). It is then fit for use, but the longer it is kept the better. I often use whole ginger instead of essence and sometimes both.

April

Easter Eggs and Elvers, Hot Cross Buns and Royal Lamprey

Easter, the celebration of *Eostre*, the Saxon goddess of Spring is an exciting mix of pagan and Christian customs and country lore, served up with traditional food. *Eostre's* feast, celebrating the Spring Equinox, always included eggs which were sacred to the Saxon goddess as symbols of re-birth after the long dead months of winter.

Many pagan rituals were adopted by the Church and tailored to fit the ecclesiastical calendar, so there are many threads of differing cultures and purpose woven into the fabric of our *holy-day* (holiday) traditions. The countryman saw it as a time for paying regard to things appertaining to both heaven and earth — the rich red soil of the Cotswolds — and no doubt squirmed impatiently in his Sunday suit as the Good Friday service dragged on, hoping that he would get on to his garden before noon to plant his potatoes and parsley, for to do so on Good Friday was to ensure good luck for the household in the coming year. Into living memory it was an unwritten rule of service that if farmworkers were not seen in church on a Good Friday they would be 'docked' — lose the wage to which they were entitled for getting to the farm even earlier than usual to do the necessary livestock feeding. Only the shepherds were exempt.

The Cotswold housewife who baked her hot cross buns before Matins was insuring against her bread going mouldy throughout the year. So, it was early rising that day. An extra bun was made as a talisman to be hung in the ingle as a protection against the house burning down, and an extra large one was hidden away to insure against illness, and if some ailment eluded its magical charm, then the bun was crumbled up and mixed into a cup of water to be drunk as a cure! One old headmaster had a hot cross bun of inestimable age — and lived to be 99!

Schoolchildren at Stratton and Baunton, near Cirencester, have enjoyed a tradition of receiving hot cross buns for several generations, and that started out as a kind of insurance, too. Butcher Abgood, landlord of The Plough at Stratton before the First World War, gave free hot cross buns to the local children as a bribe to stop them knocking his haycocks down in the paddock. The tradition was halted temporarily for the duration of World War II due to rationing, and has continued ever since. Mike and Jean Gardner, present mine hosts of The Plough, carried on the custom which they had enjoyed as local children and now, on the eve of their retirement from the pub, have ensured its continuation through the Stratton Association. As true Cotswold folk they are anxious to maintain the age-old customs of the area, and have cheerfully stood the expense of providing some 13 dozen buns a year to do so.

The spiced bun was always the subject of superstition. In the Middle Ages, bakers marked their bread with a cross to ward off the evil eye and to encourage it to rise. The custom was declared 'popish' at the Reformation, and only the buns made on Good Friday were allowed to be crossed, symbolic of the Crucifixion. Home made buns are so good they are well worth the trouble to make; they are best eaten fresh, of course, but because they are made with an enriched yeast mixture they freeze well, and are quite delicious toasted.

The end of Lenten frugality was always marked by a feast, starting gradually with fish and leavened bread on Good Friday. Herbs and spices, a feature of the Jewish Passover, are to be found in ancient recipes for Easter dishes. In the Cotswolds, the customary Easter meal was of roast lamb and egg custards. Easter Monday is celebrated in Gloucestershire Severnside villages by the world elver-eating championship. Millions of elvers, tiny young eels, make their way across the Atlantic from the Sargasso sea to their ancestral Severn in enormous 'eel-fare' — great transparent strings. Elver fishing is a traditional craft in its own right, with a language, tradition and tools peculiar to its fascinating history and skill. Many relics of the fishing equipment and memorabilia are preserved in the Folk Museum at Gloucester. The traditional method of catching (rather than fishing) the elvers is by netting them at dusk in a specially designed net of cheesecloth at ebb tide by lamplight.

The Severn also produces fine salmon, but it was the lamprey which was always the 'royal fish' of these waters — a jawless cannibalistic creature that sucks in other fish, known as 'nine eyes' because of its gill markings. It was the most highly-prized delicacy from the Middle Ages to Victorian times, and a lamprey pie was sent from the Corporation of Gloucester each year to the reigning monarch. A recipe from the Harleian Manuscript describes how this scaleless, eel-like fish with its rich flesh of delicate taste was prepared in 1450. This was also for a pie — *coffyn*, or *coffin*, being the term for a pastry case. I purposely give it here, rather than with the up-dated traditional recipe, as the method of preparation would surely have no place in today's kitchen!

Make a faire round coffyn of paste and take a fresshe lamprey. Let him blood in a vessel, and let him dye in ye same bloode. Take browne brede and stepe it in vinegar. And thereto ye same bloode and powder camel til hit be browne. Add thereto salt, peppir and a littul wyne. Then skald ye lamprey and put him in ye coffyn and caste ye sauce all round about him till he be covered. And then cover ye coffyn and seal it with a lydde above, save a littul hole. And at ye hole blow in the coffyn a good blaste of wynde and suddenly stoppe up ye hole so that ye wynde abide in ye coffyn that he falle not adown. And let bake enough and serve it forthe colde.

It conjures up a wonderful picture of the cook blowing into the pie through the 'littul hole' so 'that he falle not adown'. The custom was revived for Queen Victoria's Diamond Jubilee, when the City of Gloucester sent a lamprey pie weighing 20 pounds to the Queen. Garnished with truffles and crayfish on gold skewers, the pie bore a white silk banner displaying the Gloucester coat-of-arms and the message: 'Royal Lamprey Pie, Gloucester's Ancient Custom from the Norman period to the Victorian Era.' Queen Elizabeth II was also sent a lamprey pie as a symbol of loyalty from the burghers of Gloucester on the occasion of her Silver Jubilee in 1977. Described as a work of art, the 12 lb pie was made by the Gloucestershire College of Education, Home Economics students.

Palm Sunday Pax Cakes

The triangular shape of Pax Cakes are symbolic of the three points of the Holy Trinity.

(Makes 12)
12 ozs puff pastry
8 ozs apricot jam
1 egg
2 tablesps icing sugar

Preheat the oven to 220°C (Gas Mark 6). Cut the pastry in half. Roll out each piece to an oblong shape about 12 inches by 8 inches. Cut into six 4-inch squares, then across each square to make a total of 24 triangles. Place 12 on a wet baking tray. Place a spoonful of jam in the centre of each. Brush the edges with beaten egg and seal another triangle on top. Brush the tops with egg, cut three short slits in each top, then bake for about 15 minutes until well risen and golden brown. When cool, dust with the icing sugar.

Easter Biscuits

These were traditional Easter gifts for friends in the Cotswolds. Tied in small bundles, they were distributed on Easter Day on the way to Matins.

4 ozs butter
3 ozs caster sugar
2 egg yolks
1 tablesp brandy
1 oz currants
6 ozs plain flour
¼ teasp salt
¼ teasp powdered cinnamon
¼ teasp mixed spice

Cream the butter and sugar together, then beat in the egg yolks one at a time. Add the brandy and currants. Sieve the spices with the flour and mix in. Knead to a dough-like consistency, then roll out on a floured board to about ¼-inch thickness. Cut into rounds. Bake on a greased sheet in a pre-heated oven at 180°C (Gas Mark 4) for about 20 minutes until golden brown. Leave to cool on a baking tray before removing with a fish slice to harden off on a wire tray. Sprinkle the tops with a fine dusting of caster sugar, if liked, before removing from the tin.

Hot Cross Buns

If, like me, you dislike the tough white strips on the buns, place narrow strips of shortcrust pastry on top, or stick to the original way and simply cut a cross fairly deep in the dough.

(Makes 12)
for the dough:
1 lb strong white bread flour
3 ozs sugar
2 ozs sultanas
1 level teasp salt
1 lemon
4 ozs currants
1 oz candied peel
2 teasps ground mixed spice
2 tablesps golden syrup
ferment:
½ oz fresh yeast
2 ozs strong white flour
about 8 fl ozs warm water
1 heaped teasp sugar
1 egg

Make the ferment first by beating the egg with enough warm water to make ½ pint liquid. Whisk in the flour, yeast and sugar. Cover and keep in a warm place for ½ hour. Rinse the dried fruit and mixed candied peel in hot water, spread on kitchen paper to dry in a warm place.

Warm a large mixing bowl and sieve the flour, salt and spice into it. Rub in the lard. Make a well in the centre and grate the rind of the lemon into it. Add the sugar then the ferment.

Draw the flour in from the sides and mix together. Knead well to form a smooth and elastic dough. Sprinkle the dried fruit mixture over and knead again to blend thoroughly. Mould into a ball, and place in a warmed and lightly greased bowl. Cover with lightly greased polythene and set to rise for about an hour in a warm place. Tip out the dough and knead vigorously on a floured board.

Cover and set to rise for a further ½ hour. Cut into 12 pieces and roll between floured hands into smooth balls, flatten very gently with the palm. Place on a greased baking tray. Cut a deep cross on each bun to within about ¼ inch from the base, cover again with the polythene and leave to rise again for another 40 minutes. Pre-heat the oven to 240°C (Gas Mark 9). Bake the buns for about 8 minutes and while baking, set the golden syrup to warm; brush it over the buns as soon as they are removed from the oven. Cool on a wire tray.

Scripture Cake

I hope you will enjoy interpreting this recipe as much as I enjoyed devising it — I could not find the old one which my grandmother used to have. The children will probably like to help solve the clues for you.

Ingredients:

1 Holy Bible
A generous helping of initiative to follow the directions which are written in order of Book, Chapter and Verse, and, where necessary, the order of word in the Verse
6 ozs Deuteronomy 32,14,1st
6 ozs Solomon 4,11,lOth
12 ozs Numbers 7,31,34th
4 ozs Revelations 6,13
2 ozs Genesis 43,11,44th

Utensils:

mixing bowl, wooden spoon, knife, spatula

Cooking time:

45-50 minutes at 180°C (Gas Mark 4)

Method:

Grease the tin then line it with greased paper
Now, Judges 8,17 Deuteronomy and Solomon together
Add Numbers
Chop and add Revelations and Genesis
Exodus 16,23

Devilled Eggs

Shell hard-boiled eggs and cut across in half. Remove the yolks and mash with salt, pepper, a shake of curry powder or cayenne pepper, a teaspoonful of finely chopped parsley and blend to a soft paste with mayonnaise. Slice off a thin layer from the base of the eggs so that they stand firmly — arrange on a bed of lettuce leaves and fill with the yolk mixture. Serve with sliced tomatoes.

Baked Eggs In Saucers

This is similar to the French *ramequin*, but as the recipe is very old, and preceded the ramekin dishes which were made specially for this type of dish, it is more fun and original to cook the eggs in saucers as the British did for generations beforehand.

(Serves 4)

4 thin slices of white bread, with crusts removed
3 ozs butter
8 eggs
4 ozs mushrooms, sliced
seasoning
4 tablesps cream

Lightly butter 4 old saucers then gently melt the remaining butter in a saucepan. Pre-heat the oven to 180°C (Gas Mark 4). Dip the bread slices in the melted butter so that both sides are coated. Hold firmly at one end to allow the excess butter to run back into the pan. Press the slices into the saucer so that they are moulded to the shape. Season lightly and bake for 5 minutes. Remove from the oven and break 2 eggs into each baked bread shell. Season the eggs again, if liked, then fry the prepared mushrooms in the remaining butter in the pan. Spoon carefully round the eggs, then dribble the cream over the top of the eggs. Bake for 8-10 minutes until the eggs are set but not hard. Serve with dainty fingers of toast.

Mutton Dormers

Small mutton pies were a traditional part of feast days where customs were celebrated outdoors. The hard hot water pastry crust makes a firmer container than shortcrust pastry — although there is nothing to stop you using shortcrust if you prefer. However, the raised pies, such as these, are that little more special using the rather more time-consuming method.

Hot water crust pastry:
(Makes 8 ozs pastry — enough for 4 small pies)
8 ozs plain flour
pinch of salt
2 ozs lard
about 4 fl ozs milk and water mixed

Warm the bowl and spoon and whatever mould you are using. Sieve the flour and salt into the warmed bowl and make a well in the middle. Put the lard and milky water in a small pan and bring it to the boil. Pour into the flour and mix quickly with a wooden spoon until a soft, elastic dough is formed. Add more boiling water if it is too dry. Turn onto a floured board and knead until smooth. Keep the dough warm while you work — in a bowl over a pan of simmering water will stop it drying out as well.

Cut into 4 equally sized pieces, then from each piece cut off a third for the lid of the pie. It is possible to buy specially hinged raised pie moulds, but they can be equally successful made by hand. Flour a jar or tin — the size you require for the pie. Place on top of the two-thirds piece of dough and mould it up the sides, pulling it up as you would if moulding clay. If you are not using a jar or tin as a mould, the pies can be moulded by hand by pressing the knuckles of two fingers (in the case of small pies) into the centre of the dough, and pulling the dough away and around from the held centre, slide the fingers upright to hold down the centre and draw the sides up as far as they will go without stretching the dough to breaking point. Remember it has got to be a firm enough case to stand on its own when filled. After filling, roll the top third into a ball in your hands and pull out to fit snugly as a lid.

For the filling:
(Make this before the pastry)
1 lb lean mutton (you can use lamb, as mutton is now almost impossible to get)
1 teasp salt
¼ teasp nutmeg
¼ teasp black pepper
1 egg yolk, beaten
6 tablesps good stock or gravy

Remove any skin or gristle from the meat and shred into small pieces (but don't mince), season, then fill the prepared pastry cases (kept warm). Pack the meat mixture down firmly and spoon over the stock or gravy. Seal the pastry lids on by moistening the edges and pinching together, then marking round the edge with a floured fork so that there is a ridged pattern. Make a small hole in the top of each pie to allow the steam to escape. Brush with the beaten egg and bake for 30-40 minutes.

Serve hot with plain potatoes and broad beans, or cold with salad or crusty bread for a substantial picnic meal.

Gloucester's Lamprey Pie

(Perhaps the simplest of many versions)

8 ozs hot water crust pastry
1 lamprey
2 ozs raisins
2 ozs cooked veal, minced
4 ozs fresh white breadcrumbs
2 ozs shredded suet
1 teasp mixed herbs, finely chopped
1 egg, beaten
seasoning
about ¼ pint good stock or wine

Wash the lamprey in plenty of warm water, rubbing salt over it several times to cleanse it well. Gut it and remove head and tail, then cut out the cartilage and the two poisonous filaments on each side of the back. Wipe thoroughly. Put in a large pan and cover with water. Bring to the boil then simmer for about 30 minutes until the flesh is cooked but not falling apart. Lift carefully out and drain. When cold, pat dry. Prepare the stuffing balls by mixing together the minced veal, suet, breadcrumbs, herbs and seasoning. Bind with a little of the egg. Make 8 balls.

Prepare the pastry mould, coil the lamprey round to fit round the outer edge, fill the middle with the forcemeat balls then scatter the raisins over the fish. Pour the stock or wine carefully over. Seal the lid on, by moistening the edges and make a hole in the top. Crimp the edges and brush over with the rest of the egg. Bake at 180°C (Gas Mark 4) for about 1 hour.

Pig in a Poke

Shoulder of pork
1 onion
1 teasp chopped sage
½ teasp chopped thyme
1 egg
1 lb self-raising flour
2 teacups fresh breadcrumbs
8 ozs shredded suet
seasoning

Get the butcher to bone the shoulder for you. Wipe and season the opening. Mix together the breadcrumbs, herbs and 2 ozs of the suet, bind together with the egg, then stuff the opening, pressing in firmly with the back of a spoon. Make a suet crust pastry with the flour, a pinch of salt and the rest of the suet, mixing with water to make a soft, not sticky, dough. Roll out on a floured board until it is large enough to completely encase the stuffed meat. Wrap it round and pinch the edges together to seal. Flour a clean white cloth and place the pastry wrapped pork in the middle. Sew up the edges and tie the ends tightly with string. Place in a large pan of boiling water and keep at a steady rolling boil for about 2 hours, replenishing the pan with boiling water at intervals to keep the 'poke' covered. Serve hot with a good rich gravy and vegetables in season.

Oldbury Tarts

These little gooseberry filled tarts were also part of the spring-time festive food. The pastry is moulded to hold the fruit (which, of course, could be any fruit in season), and therefore similar to raised pie method — using boiling water to mix, rather than the softer shortcrust pastry which relies entirely on cold utensils and hands for its lightness.

1 lb self-raising flour
4 ozs butter or margarine
4 ozs lard about
4 tablesps boiling water
1½ lbs gooseberries, washed, topped and tailed
1 egg, beaten
6 ozs demerara sugar

Pre-heat the oven to 200°C (Gas Mark 6). Sift the flour into a bowl and make a well in the centre. Shred the fats into the well, then pour in the boiling water. Stir with a knife until the fats are dissolved then draw in the flour from the edges and mix to a soft dough. Cut into 8 pieces. Cut a third off each piece and reserve for the lids. Roll out the larger pieces into rounds, about the size of a small saucer. Turn the edges upwards for about an inch. Pack the prepared gooseberries in the bottom of the pastry shell. Sprinkle with sugar. Roll out the lid and seal together by pinching the edges, then twisting slightly to make a fluted border. Stand on a baking sheet, brush with the egg and make a slit in the top to allow the steam to escape. Bake for 35-40 minutes until golden brown and cooked on the bottom side. Serve hot or cold.

Baked Egg Custard

This is a rich custard made with eggs and cream and bears no resemblance to the 'boughten' custard based on cornflour for its thickening agent. It is also the base for Crême Caramel and Burnt Cream (or Brulée as it is often called). By any other name, it is well worth the trouble and despite using cream for its richness, is quite economical for a special pudding.

(Serves 4 well, or 6 smaller helpings)
½ pint milk (not skimmed)
½ pint double cream
1 vanilla pod
4 eggs
2 ozs granulated sugar
about ½ nutmeg, grated (optional)

Pre-heat the oven to 170°C (Gas Mark 3). Put the cream, milk and vanilla pod in a pan and heat gently until it just reaches the bubbling edge point below boiling. Remove from the heat and take out the vanilla pod — it can be washed, dried and used again. Beat the eggs together with the sugar lightly in a bowl and pour on the heated cream. Whisk for a minute or two then strain through a nylon sieve, to remove the egg white threads, into a lightly buttered dish. Grate the nutmeg over (if used). Stand the dish in a baking tin containing enough hot water to come three parts up the side of the dish. Bake for about an hour until set. Serve hot or cold.

Fanny Mustow's Crême Caramel

Ingredients and method as for Baked Egg Custard, but first make the caramel by dissolving 4 ozs granulated sugar in 2 tablespoons of water in a thick based pan over a low heat. Now bring to the boil quickly, and continue at boiling point without stirring until the syrup is a golden brown colour. Take a 2 pint sized ovenproof basin and pour in the caramel. Use a cloth or oven gloves as the basin will get very hot. Swirl the caramel around until the base and sides are well coated. Pour in the egg custard and bake as instructed. Allow to get cold, chill and serve, inverted on a pretty dish.

Burnt Cream (and Fruit Brulée)

Make the egg custard and leave to chill thoroughly. Sprinkle the top with soft, light brown sugar until it is quite thickly coated and covered completely to the edge. Put under a hot grill until the sugar caramelises and starts to bubble. Make sure that it does not burn (despite its name). Remove from the heat, cool quickly and chill before serving.

To make Fruit Brulée simply cover the bottom of the dish with soft fruits in season, or mix tinned fruits in the winter, cover with the egg custard and proceed as for Burnt Cream. Decorate with a spray of frosted fruits or a sprig of lemon balm or borage.

Egg Pie Pudding

8 ozs fresh breadcrumbs
1 oz soft brown sugar
chopped dates
3 eggs, whisked
4 ozs currants, or finely
about ¼ teacup red wine

Mix the dry ingredients together, then beat in the eggs, followed by the wine. Pour into a thickly buttered pie dish. Sprinkle with a few more breadcrumbs, if liked, or a few finely ground nuts, and a little butter shaved over the top. Bake at 200°C (Gas Mark 6) for about 30 minutes until firm and golden brown. Serve with pouring custard or single cream.

Gloucestershire Elvers

The elver-eating contest on Easter Monday has been a tradition at Frampton in Gloucestershire for so long that no one seems to remember the origin of it. Once upon a time almost every village on the banks of the Severn held an elver-eating competition and millions of the tiny young eels have been gulped down to the cheering and goading of the contestants' friends and neighbours. As many as a thousand of these tiny fish can make up a pound, and the skilful elver-eater can down that number in a minute. For those in less hurry, and for whom the elver season is a treat to be savoured, the traditional way of deep-frying in seasoned flour is yet to be bettered.

(Serves 4)
1 lb elvers
1 heaped tablesp flour
seasoning
oil for deep-frying
1 lemon

Wash the elvers by placing in a colander and running cold water through them several times. Place the flour and seasoning in a polythene bag, shake to mix, then add the elvers. Twist the top and shake thoroughly to coat. Deep fry in hot oil until just crisp. Serve with wedges of lemon and thin slices of bread and butter.

Egg'n Bacon Elvers

(Serves 4)
1 lb elvers
2 ozs lard
8 rashers of streaky bacon, de-rinded
3 eggs, beaten

Wash the elvers thoroughly in salted water. Drain and dry. Melt the lard in a large frying pan and fry the rashers until crisp. Remove and arrange the bacon round the edge of a warmed serving dish. Add the elvers to the hot fat in the pan and stir over a moderate heat until they go white. This takes less than a minute and overcooking spoils the elvers, so have everything to hand before you start. As soon as the elvers are cooked, pour the beaten egg over them and stir together over a moderate heat until the egg has just set. Season and pile in the centre of the dish, serve at once.

Granny's Gooseberry Mint

1 lb gooseberries
1 lb granulated sugar
about 6 fl ozs white vinegar
2 large bunches of mint

Cook the gooseberries over a gentle heat together with the vinegar and one bunch of mint, until the skins of the gooseberries are soft but the fruit still whole. Remove the mint. Add the sugar and allow to dissolve slowly. Bruise the second bunch of mint with the butt end of a rolling pin then chop roughly before adding to the fruit. Cook gently until thickened and of a chutney consistency, but do not overcook or you will lose the fresh green colour. Pot as for chutney and cover with brown paper. This keeps very well and is very good with lamb.

Lemon Curd

This delicious tangy conserve (which has a short life due to the fresh eggs in it — so keep in the refrigerator) is derived from the 17th century curd tart filling, known as cheesecakes.

(Makes 1½-2 lb)
4 medium or 3 large lemons
5 eggs
8 ozs butter
1 lb caster sugar

Grate the rind of the well washed fruit (to remove the waxy preservative) and squeeze the juice into a basin over a saucepan of boiling water. Beat the eggs gently with a fork until well-blended in a separate basin. Add the butter and sugar to the basin over the saucepan and stir until the sugar has dissolved completely. Remove from the heat and strain the beaten eggs into the mixture. Return to a low heat and cook steadily until the curd thickens and coats the back of a wooden spoon. Allow to cool a little before potting in warmed jars, and seal when cold. The curd is ready to eat immediately. Orange curd is made in exactly the same way, substituting oranges for lemons.

Badminton Cup

1 bottle red Burgundy
2 bottles soda water
2 oranges
1 level tablesp caster sugar
1 wineglass Curaçoa
½ cucumber, thinly sliced

Mix together the Burgundy and sugar, the thinly pared peel of one orange, and the juice of both, in a large jug. Place the jug in a bowl of ice cubes and leave for an hour, cover the jug with a cloth while chilling. To serve, strain into a serving jug, add the cucumber slices and the soda water to personal taste.

St George he was for England
And, before he killed the dragon
He drank a pint of English Ale
Out of an English flagon

In the days of good St George, England only had ale to give courage to dragon killers. Ale was made from heather, ground ivy, speedwell or yarrow until the Tudor period when the use of hops was introduced for making the national drink. Hop ale was at first viewed with caution, and ale was retained as the name for the old drink; beer for the new one of hops. Herbalists furthered the virtues of the new beer and it has remained in favour ever since. The Cotswolds still has a private brewery set on a millstream at Donnington, serving a string of 'proper' pubs along the valley. The recipe for Donnington ale is a family secret, of course, but this recipe is a straightforward one for the home ale or beer maker.

Home Brewed Beer

2 ozs dried hops
2 lbs malt extract
1½ lbs sugar
3 gallons freshly drawn water
1 oz yeast

Boil the hops in 1½ gallons of the water for ½ hour. Strain through muslin into a crock into which the sugar and malt extract have been placed. Stir until the sugar is dissolved. Add the rest of the water and leave until lukewarm, then add the dried yeast. Cover with a cloth, weighted with a flat board and leave to ferment for 6 days. Siphon off into screw-top bottles, adding 1 teasp of sugar to each bottle before sealing. Leave for 2 weeks before drinking.

May

Whit Wake Cheeses and Wap Whipot

May Day was once as important as Christmas in country calendars, more so, of course, in pre-Christian times when pagan ritual heralded in the seasons, and today the maypole remains the enduring symbol of those early May Day celebrations. Right across the Cotswolds May Day has been celebrated in some form or other: at Magdalen College, Oxford, choristers greet the day as dawn breaks from the top of the tower, with the Latin hymn, *Te Deum Patrem colimus*, which is part of the College Grace and is 17th century, but the custom is thought to date back at least to the time of Henry VII. More down to earth customs prevailed on the hills and in the vales where May Walking, gathering summer greenery and flowers to bedeck homes, lingered into this century at Minchinhampton. Knocking up the trees has had a revival at Birdlip in recent years and village schools have incorporated maypole dancing in their country dancing programmes, keeping the tradition alive.

It is the customs of the Wakes, or Patronal Feasts, known in the Cotswolds as Revels, which have stood the test of time and make May a merry month.

Whit Ales were originally means of fund-raising for the church and often referred to as Church Ales, providing alms for the poor, helping with maintenance costs of the church itself and providing a popular social occasion for the parishioners in the days before rates were introduced. The famous *Cotswold Olympick Games*, or Dover's Games as they are often called, after their founder, Robert Dover, were first instituted in Whit week in 1612 and extended the Whitsun Ale into Revels of sporting games such as hare-coursing, shin-kicking, jousting and breaking heads with cudgels just for the fun of it, with a sprinkling of lighter pursuits such as dancing and card games for the weaker in strength and spirit. Dover's Games and Scuttlebrook Wake are still very much a part of the Cotswold scene.

As far as festive food is concerned, it is to the Cooper's Hill Wake that we have to go for the annual cheese-rolling, the origin of which is a mixture of ancient beliefs and superstition. It could be that the custom of chasing down a one-in-one gradient after a sunshine-coloured cheese derived from a ritual of trying to arrest the sun in an annual saturnalia; more practical folks declare the custom to be one of establishing grazing rights on the common. Whatever the origin, the celebration of Spring Bank Monday (formerly Whitsuntide) at Cooper's Hill, Brockworth, is one of the few cheeserolling ceremonies left in the kingdom and a highlight of the Cotswold calendar. The cheeses are as famous as the tradition — Double Gloucester, of course, itself a unique cheese made in traditional style by the last of the great Gloucester Vale cheesemakers.

A handbill sent to the Town Crier of Gloucester to 'cry' the annual sports of Whitsuntide 1836, gives a fascinating glimpse of the country fun and junketings of those days:

Cooper's Hill Weke to commence
on Wits Monday
persisly at 3 o'clock.
2 cheese to be ron for
1 Plain Cake to be green for
1 do. do. to be jumpt in the bag for
Horings to be Dipt in the toob for

Set of ribons to be dansed for
Shimey to be ron for
Belt to be rosled for
A bladder of snuff to be
chatred for by hold wimming

The grinning (through a horse's collar) and wrestling and dancing and chattering by old women have been replaced by tug-of-war and scrambling for sweets from the maypole. But the cheeses are still 'ron' for, and there are always plenty of brave contestants to chase the 71b Double Gloucesters down the notoriously steep hill, risking life and limb to uphold an ancient Cotswold tradition.

Cheese-rolling has more ecclesiastical connotations in the Stroud valley village of Randwick. Here, on the first Sunday in May (it used to be on May Day in ancient times), three Double Gloucester cheeses are rolled three times round the parish church anticlockwise by those present forming a ring. The cheese, from the rolling, is cut up and distributed at Randwick Wap.

Runnick Wap, as it was locally known, survives today as a country fair, the highlight of which is the ancient Mayor-making ceremony — with High Sheriff, Swordbearer, Mopman, a Wap Queen and attendants, and the cheeses carried on a flower-decked litter during a colourful and fun-filled day held now on the second Saturday in May. Gloucestershire's great historian, Samuel Rudder, wrote of the Wap in the late 18th century as 'an ancient custom'. It survived the puritanical suppression of lively revels and wakes with their licence for intemperance; as did a custom at Childswickham *'from time immemorial'. Rudder's description of that village's Wake is interesting insofar as it gives us a look at the fare of his day: 'The Lord of the Manor gives a certain quantity of malt to brew ale to be given away at Whitsuntide and a certain quantity of flour to make cakes; everyone who keeps a cow sends curds, others plums, sugar and flour; and the payers to church' and poor contribute 6d each towards furnishing out an entertainment, to which every poor person of the parish who comes, has, with a quart of ale, a cake, a piece of cheese, and a cheesecake.'*

Cheesecakes for Whitsun Ales were mentioned as early as 1634 when a miller at Churchdown 'made large preparation (for 'a solemn' Whitsun Ale) even of threescore dozen cheesecakes'. Probably the earliest mention of cheesecake is one of 1265 when soft curds were listed for tarts. Curd cheesecakes, probably of ewe's milk, was a staple diet for Cotswold shepherds at shearing time. Curd cheese gives a richer cheesecake, but cottage cheese can be used instead, but should be sieved first. Originally the cheesecake was a mixture of pounded curds, egg yolks and spices with honey. Later, dried fruit was added and over the centuries so many variations have been made that cheesecake often contains no cheese at all, and is only recognised as the biscuit-base creamy set cheesecake which originated on the other side of the Atlantic. By Elizabethan times it was established as a sweet pie — and the recipe here fits therefore into the puddings section, whereas another traditional baked cheesecake is more cake-like so I have put it with the cakes. So, we have a cheesecake which is really a pudding and a Gloucester Cheese Pudding which is really not a pudding in the sweets or desserts sense, but a savoury supper dish. If that is not all confusing enough, there is always the White Pot — which, even in John Smith's (or Smyth's) day - the 17th century — there appears to have been some variation on the theme of traditional Cotswold cooking!

Hee is very good at white pott. By white pot,
wee westerners doe meane a great custard or
puddinge baked in a bagg, platter, kettle or
pan: notinge heerby, a good trencher man, or
great eater.

It was reported in the local newspaper that when the mail coach brought the news of the end of the Boer War it was met with 'but a tardy reception' in the Coln Valley, 'as the May fly was up'. The popularity of fresh trout has increased to the extent that trout farms have been introduced in the Cotswolds so that visitors can catch their own, without waiting for the 'May fly to be up'. However, it is appropriate that the selection of May recipes should start with Cotswold river trout as a salute to the time-honoured tradition.

Corn-Husk Baked Trout

This is an ideal way to barbecue freshly-caught trout, but it can also be cooked in an oven, or wrapped in foil if corn-husks are not available. The corn cob can be boiled, or barbecued, and served — liberally spread with butter — with the trout.

(Serves 4)
4 fresh rainbow trout
2 ozs softened butter
8 rashers unsmoked bacon
4 bay leaves (crushed)
2 teasps lemon juice
1 tablesp finely chopped parsley
1 teasp dried marjoram
1 lemon (for garnish)
4 cobs of corn
seasoning

Remove the cobs of corn from the husks and wipe inside the husks. Clean and gut the trout. Pound the butter, bay leaves, lemon juice and seasoning together and divide into 4 pieces. Place a portion of the butter inside each trout and season well, sprinkle on the marjoram then wrap each in two rashers of bacon and place inside the corn husk. Tie securely at the silk end. Bake in glowing embers, if barbecue is used, or in a very hot oven, for about 9 minutes, turning the trout parcels over and cooking for the same time on the other side. Test whether the fish is cooked by flaking the flesh with a fork; it should flake easily. Serve immediately with a quarter of the lemon to each trout.

Coln Valley Paté

About 2 lbs fresh trout
4 ozs farm butter
3 ozs field mushrooms
dash of anchovy sauce
seasoning

Clean the trout, but do not remove the heads. Spread a sliver of the butter inside each fish, wrap in foil and steam over a pan of boiling water for 35 minutes. While the fish is cooking prepare the mushrooms. After peeling them and cleaning the stalks chop small and fry in about an ounce of the butter until softened. When the trout is cooked, drain any residue of butter from the paper into a basin and carefully flake the flesh into it. Discard the skin, heads and bones. Add the fried mushrooms with any liquid left in the pan and beat well with a fork until well broken down. Add a dash of anchovy sauce and season to taste. Melt the remaining butter and add just enough to bind the mixture together. Pack into small pots and pour the remaining melted butter over the top to make a thin seal. Leave to set in a cool place then cover with cling film. The paté will keep for about a fortnight in the fridge. Serve on toast, or use as a sandwich spread.

Gloucester Cheese Paté Roll

4 ozs Double Gloucester cheese — this is better when hard rather than just freshly bought
4 ozs soft cheese — home-made curd cheese, if liked
finely grated rind of half a lemon
2 tablesps finely chopped fresh chives

Grate the Double Gloucester cheese into a bowl, add the soft cheese, lemon rind and half the chives. Beat well until smooth. Spoon the rest of the chives evenly onto a sheet of greaseproof paper, then pile the cheese mixture in the centre. Using the paper, roll the cheese into a neat fat sausage shape so that it is well covered with chives. Fold the paper over loosely and chill for a couple of hours to firm up. Transfer to a serving dish and cut into slices to serve with fresh rolls and salad and, or, jacket potato.

Vale Special Soup

The two main ingredients for this delicious soup combine the specialities of the lush vales at the foot of the Cotswold hills: the full-bodied cheese from the Vale of Gloucester and the delicate taste of asparagus grown in the fertile Vale of Evesham.

(Serves 4)
One bunch of fresh asparagus
8 ozs cooked potato
4 tablesps soured cream
½ pint milk
1 ½ pints chicken stock or clear vegetable stock)
4 ozs mature cheese (Double Gloucester for choice) grated
2 slices of bread

Cook the asparagus until tender, chop into a bowl and mix with the potato, soured cream and milk. Purée in a blender then tip into a saucepan, adding the stock and stirring well over a gentle heat. Do not allow to boil. Toast the bread while the soup is heating through, scatter half the grated cheese over the toast and put under a hot grill to bubble and brown. Stir the rest of the cheese into the soup, season to taste and as soon as the cheese is melted into the soup, serve with the toast cut into small squares floating on the top of each dish.

Curds and Whey

Home-made curd cheese has a lovely soft and creamy texture and is very little trouble to make. When I was a child we used to make the curd cheese from milk that had naturally soured, so it was always part of hot summer memories. Today, because pasteurised milk has been heat treated to give it a longer life, the natural souring bacteria has been killed, so pasteurised milk has to be soured by lemon juice to work on the protein and calcium in the milk to separate the clotting curds from the thin watery whey. The little white muslin bags hanging from the cup hooks in the dark larder, dripping the whey into a china dish, was one of the magical metamorphoses which stimulated my passion for cooking at a very early age.

This home-made curd cheese has many uses as an ingredient, but is equally good eaten on its own as a spread or filling; the whey is a nice drink if chilled first.

To make 4-5 ozs curd cheese

1 pint fresh milk (not long-life treated — UHT type)
3 tablesps lemon juice
2 tablesps single cream or top of the milk

Heat the milk to blood heat (38°C/100°F). Pour into a bowl and add the lemon juice. Leave to stand in a warm place for 30 minutes after which time you should be able to see that the curds have separated from the whey. Line a sieve with a square of butter muslin (a clean J-cloth will do). Pour the curds and whey through the lined sieve over the bowl. Tie the corners together and hang over the bowl to drain for at least an hour. Scrape the curd from the cloth and put into a clean bowl, mix in the top of the milk or cream and it is ready to use. If liked it can be seasoned and all kinds of additions made, such as finely chopped chives, herbs, shreds of pineapple, prawns, ham, grated onion, finely chopped pepper or cucumber — the variation is immense.

Pear And Cheese Prelude

This is a simple starter, light and fresh before a main course.

(Serves 4)

4 ripe pears (or 8 halves if using tinned — well drained)
4 ozs curd cheese
2 ozs walnuts
small lettuce
a few chives, finely snipped
2 tablesps light salad dressing

Line a serving dish with half the lettuce leaves, finely shred the remainder and make four little 'nests'. Halve and core the pears if using fresh and spoon a little hollow out of each. Heap curd cheese into each hollow, shaping neatly, spoon over the dressing of choice, scatter with chives and finish with walnut halves.

Cotswold Village Trout

I have named this method of cooking trout as a tribute to J Arthur Gibbs, author of the classic *A Cotswold Village*, who said: 'out of this fairy spring was taken quite recently, but not with the 'dry' fly — for no fish could be deceived in water of such stainless transparency — a trout that weighed three pounds and a half. He was far and away the most beautiful trout I ever saw; as silvery as salmon that has just left the sea, he was a worthy denizen of the secluded depths of that crystal spring, still welling up from the pure limestone rock in the heart of the Cotswold Hills, as it has for a thousand years.'

To create a dish to illustrate the young squire's description of the spring-fed pool close to Ablington Manor House where he lived at the end of the last century, I researched into the cooking methods of earlier days, and adapted a late medieval recipe for freshwater fish —in which they were set in jelly. If you set a few fronds of fennel on the serving dish first then the scene is set of the fern-like Cotswold stream bottom in which the trout lie.

(Serves 6)

6 trout (of about 8 ozs weight each) gutted and cleaned
1 carrot, sliced
¼ pint dry white wine
1 tablesp white wine vinegar
6 peppercorns
1 onion, sliced thinly
pinch of salt
1 bay leaf
2 sprigs each of parsley and thyme

Put the wine, vinegar, herbs, vegetables and seasoning into a pan with ¾ pint of water, cover with a lid and bring to the boil. Reduce the heat and simmer for 30 minutes. Cool. Place the trout in a pan in which they fit snugly. Strain the cooled stock over and bring gently to boiling point. Reduce the heat and simmer for about 10 minutes. Test if done, the flesh should be easily flaked by a fork. Remove the fish carefully and when cool enough to handle, remove the skin, heads and backbones and put them back in the pan of stock in which the trout were cooked. Bring the stock to the boil and keep at a full simmering roll until reduced down to about half. Lay the trout fillets neatly on a serving dish which is at least an inch deep. Lay a few fronds of fennel alongside the fish, then strain the liquid over. Leave to set overnight in the fridge or cold larder. The jelly will set to a clear amber like sunlight striking a Cotswold stream!

Cotswold Cheese Casserole

This is an excellent way to enjoy early potatoes, choose small even sized ones.

(Serves 4)
1½ lbs new potatoes, boiled
1 oz butter
3 stalks of celery, finely chopped
4 new carrots, grated
4 ozs plain yoghurt
1 tablesp mayonnaise
6 ozs Double Gloucester cheese, grated

As soon as the potatoes are cooked, strain off the water and add the butter to the hot pan, toss gently to coat the potatoes. Add the rest of the ingredients, except the cheese, and reheat but do not boil. Turn into a casserole dish and spread the cheese thickly over the top. Brown under a very hot grill until the cheese bubbles and turns golden, serve immediately with thick hunks of buttered crusty bread, a green salad and a dish of sliced onion and tomato rings.

Herby Curd Cheesecake

(Serves 6)
4 ozs cream cracker biscuits
2 ozs butter
6 ozs curd cheese
6 ozs hard cheese, grated
3 eggs, beaten
5 fl ozs natural set yoghurt
1 small onion, finely chopped
2 sticks celery, finely chopped
parsley, dill and chives
1 level tablesp each of chopped
seasoning

Set the oven to 180°C (Gas Mark 4). Put the crackers into a plastic bag and crush with a rolling pin. Melt the butter in a small pan and add the biscuit crumbs. Mix well then tip into a buttered and paper-lined 8-inch spring clip tin, pressing down to cover the base firmly. Beat the cheeses, yoghurt and eggs together, fold in the rest of the ingredients and pour over the biscuit crumb base. Bake in the centre of the oven for about an hour until set and the top golden brown. Serve warm or cold, garnished with fresh herbs, with salad.

Curdcake Sweet Pye

(Serves 6)
6 ozs shortcrust pastry
2 ozs butter
3 ozs caster sugar
2 eggs — separated
2 level teasps cornflour
8 ozs curd (or cottage) cheese
grated rind of one lemon

Preheat the oven to 190°C (Gas Mark 5) while rolling out the pastry to line an 8-inch flan tin. Fill with lightly crumpled foil and bake blind for 12 minutes. Remove the foil and continue baking the pastry case for another 4 minutes. Remove from oven to cool while making the filling. Lower the oven heat to 180°C (Gas Mark 4). Beat together the butter and sugar until light and fluffy, then beat in the egg yolks one at a time. Fold in the cornflour, curd cheese, sultanas and lemon rind until the mixture is smooth and well blended. Whisk the egg whites to a stiffly peaking stage and fold into the cheese mixture. Spoon into the pastry case and bake for about 30 minutes until firm and golden brown. Serve hot or cold.

Gloucestershire Apple Pie

'An apple pie without the cheese, is like a kiss without the squeeze' is an old Cotswold saying, and I remember my Granny slipping a sliver of cheese under the crust when she made apple pie — just to appease Grampy Lewis. This recipe is for a deep pie with a lattice top, in which cheese is mixed with the apple.

(Serves 8)
8 ozs wholemeal flour
4 ozs flour
6 ozs butter
1½ lbs cooking apples, prepared
3 ozs brown sugar
2 ozs walnuts, chopped
6 ozs Double Gloucester cheese
1 egg
½ teasp ground nutmeg

Make the pastry by rubbing the butter into the mixed flours until it is breadcrumb-like in texture. Mix with enough cold water to form a soft dough. Let it rest in a cool place while preparing the filling and pre-heating the oven to 200°C (Gas Mark 6). Chop the apples into cubes and heat in a pan with the sugar and nutmeg until softened. Roll out the pastry and line a greased 8-inch deep pie dish or flan tin. Cube the cheese and arrange evenly in the pastry case with the apple, sprinkle with the walnuts. Roll out the pastry trimmings and cut into strips. Twist each strip lightly and arrange over the filling in a lattice pattern, pinching the joining edges against the side. Brush with the egg, lightly beaten, and bake for about 35 minutes until cooked and golden. Serve hot or cold with custard, or ice cream.

Cheesecake Bake

This is more like a fairly solid cheese custard and is adapted from a very old recipe which pre-dates the cooking range and pastry dishes. It is interesting to know that it is very similar to Russian Cheesecake.

(Serves 4)
1 lb curd or cottage cheese
1 ½ ozs butter, melted
2 level tablesps semolina or ground rice
pinch of salt
4 tablesps raisins
1 egg
4 tablesps sugar
¼ pint soured cream
1 teasp vanilla essence (optional)

Pre-heat the oven to 190°C (Gas Mark 5). Beat the cheese in a bowl until quite smooth. Mix in the rest of the ingredients and beat well. Spoon into a buttered ovenproof dish — or small individual dishes — and smooth the top. Spoon over the soured cream. Bake at the top of the oven for 25-30 minutes until set. Serve hot or cold.

Quick Cheesecake

This is the biscuit base cheesecake which we have come to accept as 'traditional'. This recipe is a good basic one which can be varied by flavouring and toppings.

(Serves 8)
6 ozs sweet biscuits, crushed
3 ozs butter, melted
12 ozs soft cheese, full-fat, curd or cottage — or mixed
½ oz gelatine (or a packet jelly, and ¼ pint water)
¼ pint whipping cream, or a mix of double and single creams to ¼ pint (or a small tin of evaporated milk)
¼ pint fruit puree

Mix the biscuit crumbs and melted butter together and press down over the base of a buttered 8-inch spring-type cake tin. Chill while preparing the filling. Dissolve the gelatine in the warmed fruit puree - or dissolve the jelly cubes in hot water. Beat the cheese(s) until soft and gradually add the jelly or gelatine mix. Whip the cream until bulky (if using evaporated milk, then chill the tin first, it makes it easier to whip), and fold into the cheese mixture. Pour over the crumb base and leave in the fridge for several hours to set.

All kinds of different flavours can be added to this basic recipe: try a spoonful of cocoa powder and the juice of a small lemon over chocolate wholemeal crumb base; add chopped fruit to the filling, or dissolve the jelly in wine and top with fresh grapes.

White Put, Pout or *Pot* obviously derived from a kind of pottage and has been made in the West Gloucestershire villages since time began to celebrate Whitsuntide Revels. There seem to be as many variations of the dish as its spelling, varying from a porridgy type of baked custard to a stick-to-your-ribs type bread pudding, to a baked sop. I cannot pretend to have made these first four recipes and include them for their historic value and for those with large families with venturesome spirits and appetites to match!

White Put (Tockington)

2 pints milk
1 egg
2 tablesps golden syrup
1 tablesp flour

Boil the milk and pour over the rest of the ingredients, mix thoroughly and bake in a pie dish in a slow over for 3 or 4 hours. Can be eaten cold or warm.

White Pot (Oldbury Style)

2 pints milk
2 tablesps treacle
1 tablesp brown sugar
1 tablesp flour
½ cup of cold water

Mix the flour, treacle and sugar together with a little cold milk. Boil the rest of the milk and pour on to the mixture, stir well and add the cold water. Bake in a slow oven for two hours.

White Pot (Dyrham Style)

4 quarts milk
1 lb flour
1 lb golden syrup
8 eggs
2 ozs butter
2 nutmegs, grated
mixed spice to taste

Have ready a deep earthenware pan. Beat into it the flour, eggs, syrup and spices. Bring the milk to the boil and at boiling point stir in the other ingredients, forming a paste. Dot the butter in pieces on the top, and at the last moment pour ¾ pint of cold water into the middle of the pan and put into the oven without stirring. The ideal oven for this is the old-fashioned farmhouse bread oven. Bake in a fairly hot oven for the first hour, then let the oven go down gradually and bake gently for 7 or 8 hours. Half quantities may be made, but always bake in a deep bowl or pan.

White Pout (Cromhall Style)

1 gallon skim milk
12 ozs patent flour (self-raising)
4 eggs
1 oz butter
sugar and spice to taste
1 teacupful cider

Mix all together until batter-like. Bake for 5 or 6 hours.

What is a tried and well-tested White Pot, however, is one which was devised by Pat Ballinger about 20 years ago when the Randwick Wap was revived. After researching into the history of the Wap and trying to decipher what made the Randwick White Pot special, she guessed that ‘the secret ingredient’ referred to was home-made wine. Bread pudding had been a Ballinger family recipe for generations and Pat adapted her mother's recipe for the Wap. Now a traditional part of the celebrations, the Randwick Whipot is made by Pat in the old fashioned deep earthenware crock and mixed by hand in the time-honoured way. Dressed in mob-cap and apron, Pat sells the Whipot in thick slices over her garden wall for funds to help with the expenses of the Wap. As soon as she rings her handbell, the villagers crowd round for a taste of good old Cotswold cooking. I am grateful to Pat for sharing this recipe with us.

Wap Whipot (Randwick Style)

1 large stale white loaf
6 ozs margarine
4 ozs self-raising flour
6 ozs granulated sugar
8 ozs mixed dried fruit
4 eggs
1 wineglassful red wine (preferably home-made)
milk to mix

Slice the bread and break into pieces. Soak in enough water to cover for at least two hours. Squeeze the water out of the bread with your hands, as dry as you can. Put into a deep crock and mix in all the other ingredients — with your hands — adding the wine and enough milk to make the mixture quite sloppy. Bake in a moderately slow oven as the long, slow baking gives a better texture, until firm and golden brown. This can be eaten warm as a pudding, or cut into slabs when cold.

Gloucester Cheese Pudding

(Serves 4)
8 ozs Double Gloucester cheese (grated)
1 oz butter
3 eggs
8 slices of wholemeal bread
1 teasp prepared English mustard
1 tablesp peanut butter (crunchy or smooth)
¾ pint fresh milk
seasoning
1 tablesp fresh parsley, finely chopped

Remove the crusts from the bread, and butter the slices. Mix together the peanut butter and half the grated cheese and make sandwiches, cutting each across diagonally to make triangles. Pack with the pointed edge upwards into a buttered ovenproof dish. Beat the eggs, milk and mustard with seasoning to taste and pour over the sandwiches. Leave for 30 minutes for the bread to absorb the liquid. Mix the rest of the cheese and the parsley together and sprinkle over the top. Bake in a pre-heated oven at 180°C (Gas Mark 4) for 40-45 minutes until set and golden brown. Serve immediately with a crisp green salad.

Gloucestershire Cheese and Ale

This dish dates back to medieval times, when it was served in the country inns as well as in the kitchens of the vast sheep farms.

(Serves 4)
4 ozs Double Gloucester cheese
4 thick slices wholemeal bread
scant teasp of made mustard (Tewkesbury if you can get it)
¼ pint strong ale

Flake the cheese (it should not be grated) into thin slivers into an ovenproof dish. Spread with the mustard then cover with the ale. Melt in a very hot oven, pre-heated to 230°C (Gas Mark 8), for 5-10 minutes. Toast the bread. Remove the cheese from the oven. If there is loose ale in the dish, spoon it on to the toast to moisten it then spread the cheese over. Serve piping hot with pickled onions and, of course, a glass of good Cotswold brewed ale.

Baked Lemon Cheesecake

Although this has a biscuit crumb base, usually associated with the set cheesecakes of our transatlantic cousins, this baked cheesecake is along the traditional lines and is more like a tea-time cake — the slight sinking and cracking when it cools is perfectly normal and due to the light texture.

(Serves 8)
4 ozs digestive biscuits, crushed
2 ozs butter
6 ozs full fat cream cheese
6 ozs cottage or curd cheese
4 ozs caster sugar
3 eggs, separated
1 lemon
2 ozs raisins
¼ pint double cream
1 oz plain flour
mean shake of mixed spice
icing sugar, to dust
(Use 12 ozs of full fat cream cheese for a richer cheesecake, if liked, instead of half and half)

Pre-heat the oven to 170°C (Gas Mark 3). Melt the butter and mix in the biscuit crumbs. Tip into a lightly buttered 8-inch spring clip cake tin. Press down firmly to cover the base. Chill while preparing the filling. Beat the cheese and caster sugar together until creamy and light, then gradually beat in the egg yolks. Add the grated rind and strained juice of the lemon and the raisins.

Whip the cream until bulky but not stiff, fold into the cheese mixture. Fold the flour, mixed with the spice, lightly through. Whisk the egg whites until softly peaking and fold them into the mixture. Pour into the tin and bake in the centre of the oven for 1¾ hours until risen and firm to the touch. Cool in the tin. Remove to a serving plate and dredge with the icing sugar.

Cheese Crackers

(Makes about 2 dozen)
6 ozs plain flour
2 ozs butter
8 ozs curd or cottage cheese
½ level teasp garlic or onion salt
pinch of cayenne pepper
1 oz sunflower seeds

Pre-heat the oven to 160 °C (Gas Mark 3). Rub the butter into the flour and mix in the rest of the ingredients, combining well until a dough-like texture is formed. Roll out on a well floured board quite thinly (about one-eighth of an inch thickness) and cut into 3-inch squares — a pastry wheel run alongside a ruler makes a neat job. Place on an ungreased baking sheet and prick with a fork. Bake for 20-25 minutes until golden and crisp. Serve with cheese or paté.

Classic Cheese Sauce

(Makes ½ pint)
½ oz butter
½ oz flour
½ pint milk
½ teasp prepared English mustard
2 ozs strong cheese, grated
seasoning to taste

Melt the butter in a saucepan, add the flour and cook over a very low heat to blend without browning. Gradually add the milk, stirring to prevent lumps. Bring slowly to the boil, and continue to cook at boiling point, stirring all the time, for 2 or 3 minutes until thickened. Remove from the heat and add the cheese, mustard and seasoning. This makes a good basic pouring sauce. If a thicker coating sauce is needed, double the quantity of butter and flour. Use for fish, poultry, ham, egg, and vegetable dishes.

Gooseberry Sauce

This is an 18th century recipe which was served with fish — particularly the rich oily mackerel — but is still delicious with the milder Coln Valley trout, the sharpness of the gooseberries giving a good contrasting flavour. Use the thinnings of the gooseberry crop for this.

(Serves 4)
12 ozs gooseberries, washed and topped and tailed
1 oz butter
1 oz sugar
½ level teasp ground nutmeg
a pinch of salt and black pepper

Boil the gooseberries in ½ pint water for about 5 minutes until tender. Purée in a liquidiser, or sieve, and return to the pan. Add the rest of the ingredients and reheat until the sugar has dissolved, but do not allow to boil.

Fromage Blanc

4 ozs plain cottage or home-made curd cheese
4 ozs natural yoghurt
2 teasps lemon juice (use fresh lemon, rather than bottled juice)

Liquidise all ingredients together into a smooth, thick, shiny cream texture. Leave covered with cling film, in a cool place for a least an hour before serving.

With the emphasis today on healthier eating there is a call to reduce the amount of dairy products such as cream. Finding a satisfying substitute devoid of artificial ingredients is almost impossible, unless you are prepared to make it yourself: This is a very good method of making a tasty alternative to cream to serve with fresh fruit salads and puddings.

Curd Cheese Salad Dressing

4 ozs curd cheese
1 clove garlic, crushed (opintional)
1 tablesp natural yoghurt (or soured cream)
1 tablesp cider vinegar

Beat or liquidise all together until smooth.

Nettle Beer

An agreeable way to enjoy your weeds — at a later date!

Young and fresh nettle tops, enough to loosely fill a small pail
3 lbs sugar
2 ozs bruised whole ginger
2 gallons cold water
1 oz dried yeast
3 small bunches of goosegrass
3 good bunches of young dandelion leaves, blackcurrant leaves or burdock

Boil the plant stuff for about ten minutes, strain on to the sugar which should be put into an earthenware crock. Stir to dissolve the sugar. When cooled to lukewarm, add the yeast and cover. Leave in a warmish place for six days. Siphon off into clean screw-top bottles and add a teaspoon of sugar to each bottle. Leave until quite cleared before drinking.

June

A Midsummer's Dream of Strawberries and Cream

Junkets and jellies and such dainty fare
May all invited freely with me share Old Song

Midsummer's fulsome fruits and flowers add colour and fragrance to the month of June, named after Juno, the wife of Jupiter. Christian and pagan festivals fall in full summer. The summit of the year, with its telling tale of the longest day, the summer solstice on the 21st, is still celebrated with the pagan rites by Druids in an air of mystery and magic. Old Midsummer Eve was somehow set for two days later, and with its roots in pagan ritual, it assumed a scriptural identity as St John's Eve. Country folk would listen hard for the cuckoo's mocking call at that time, for to hear its song after that day foretold a late harvest.

As was the wont of the countryman, the weather portents and farming calendar were fitted snugly into easy-to-remember couplets:

On St Barnabus'
Put the scythe to the grass
Barnaby bright, Barnaby bright.
Longest day, shortest night.
If St Vitus' day be rainy weather
It will rain for forty days together

St Barnabus' Day, on June 11th, was reckoned, as the old rhyme tells, the date for starting the hay-making. And to keep faith with the old country customs I have included a recipe using hay in the cooking itself! St Vitus' Day, on the 15th, was important for forecasting the soft fruit season. The Cotswolds now have many fruit farms where you can go and pick your own strawberries and raspberries, so after a couple of hours in the summer sunshine picking the fruit it is a pleasure to use the warm sweet smelling berries in the kitchen to make delicious dishes. Before the days of the fruit farm, the tiny upland village of Clapton-on-the-Hill, formerly called Clapton super Montibus, was known locally as 'strawberry village'. And the small sweet wild strawberry grows all over the Cotswolds in the wooded valleys. My favourite story about Cotswold strawberries is the one Sir John Dorrington related from an entry in the diary of Thomas Gardner.

George III, his Queen, and some of his children, visited Cranham or the neighbourhood in July 1788. A very aged woman, who did not know who her visitors were, came from her cottage door and presented the old gentleman and his Lady with a dish of bright red fragrant woodland strawberries. The old gentleman graciously accepted the welcome present. The dish was quickly cleared of its simple luxury.

The old woman stood by for her dish, and curtsied most respectfully and politely when it was returned. The old woman imagined it was the Squire and his family come to live at the great house. As the old woman held out her hand to receive the empty dish, the gentleman said in a most polite and affectionate manner, 'I am very much obliged to you for your great kindness.' You be mortal welcome.' replied the old woman, 'but I don't know who ye be — the Squire I spose?' 'No, my good woman, I have left my picture on the dish.'

The carriage drove back towards Cheltenham, and the woman returned to her cottage. When she put her empty dish upon the her cottage table, she saw a 'golden guinea' glittering on the plate. 'I thought he said he had put his pic'tur on the dish. Well, I never know'd such a thing. This be a pretty pic'tur'.

Chilled Cucumber Soup

Deliciously refreshing for a hot summer's meal. This soup also freezes well.

(Serves 6)
1 cucumber
1 onion, finely chopped
8 ozs peeled and finely diced potatoes
½ pint milk
1 tablesp fresh mint, chopped finely
seasoning
1 pint good vegetable stock
1 tablesp sunflower oil
¼ pint single cream and a bunch of fresh mint for garnish

Heat the oil gently in a large pan and cook the onions and potatoes together for about 13 minutes over a low heat with the lid on. Wipe the cucumber, cut in half lengthwise and remove the seeds, chop the flesh roughly and add to the pan. Cook for about 3 minutes, then stir in the chopped mint, the stock and the milk, blending together. Bring quickly to the boil then reduce the heat immediately and simmer for 30 minutes. Remove from the heat and sieve or liquidise until smooth. If some texture is preferred, then liquidise half the soup until smooth and only give the remainder a short burst and mix together. Season to taste, cool as quickly as possible then chill thoroughly. At the point of serving, add a couple of crushed ice cubes, stir through the soup, pour into serving dishes, then swirl the cream on top. Garnish with fresh mint leaves.

Egg Mousse

A light starter for summer

3 hard boiled eggs, shelled
1 tablesp mayonnaise
½ pint chicken or vegetable stock
¼ oz gelatine (2 teasps)
1 tablesp whipped cream
pinch of mild curry powder
seasoning
chopped parsley for garnish

Sieve the eggs, add mayonnaise and curry powder, season to taste. Dissolve the gelatine in the stock and stir in. Leave to just setting point, then stir in the whipped cream and pour into a lightly oiled mould to set. Serve inverted onto a pretty dish and scatter chopped parsley over.

Hay Baked Lamb

This is a really old method for cooking lamb which is no longer young! If you cannot get fresh, sweet-smelling hay from the farm, it is possible to buy it from pet shops. Don't worry about creepy crawlies — they don't survive the oven temperature and long baking.

Leg of (older) lamb about 4 lb
4 cloves of garlic, peeled and cut in half
8 sprigs of rosemary tips
3 ozs butter
¼ pint red wine
about 6 ozs clean hay
2 tablesps chopped parsley and chives and mint, mixed
seasoning — use coarse salt and freshly ground black pepper for choice

Wipe the lamb and make little slits equally spaced in the skin, insert the garlic pieces and rosemary tips together into each incision. Spread the butter over the joint and scatter the chopped herbs all over. Press down the herbs onto the butter, and season.

Line a baking dish with foil and spread half the hay over. Lay the leg of lamb on top and cover with the rest of the hay. Pour the wine over the hay to soak through to the lamb, then cover the whole top with a sheet of foil. Bake in a pre-heated oven at 220°C (Gas Mark 8) for about 2 hours. Remove the foil and hay, take the lamb off its bed of hay, and scrape off any bits which have stuck

January

above: Pitchfork Chutney (page 15)
left: Week-spiced Beef (page 10)

February

above: Love Apple Soup (page 17)
right: Pan-on Pancakes (page 20)

March

top: Simnel Cake (page 28)
left: Honeyed Lamb in Cider (page 26)

April

above: Burnt Cream and Fruit Brulée (page 36)
right: Granny's Gooseberry Mint (page 37)

to it. Place on a warmed serving dish and allow to rest for 10-15 minutes before carving. Serve with roast potatoes, green vegetables and onion sauce and redcurrant jelly, or jacket potatoes and salad.

Salmon With Orange Sauce

(Serves 4)
4 salmon steaks (about 4-5 ozs each)
1 large orange
1 teasp cornflour
½ teasp cinnamon
1 teasp demerara sugar
¼ pint buttermilk (or natural yoghurt)

Pre-heat the oven to 190°C (Gas Mark 5). Wash and dry the salmon steaks and place each on a square of foil which has been very lightly oiled. Fold the edges tightly to form a leakproof parcel. Put on a baking sheet and cook for about 15 minutes when the salmon flesh should look opaque. Keep warm on a dish while making the sauce. Grate the rind of the orange and put into a small pan with the juice, sugar and cinnamon, mix in the cornflour to a smooth paste and add the buttermilk or yoghurt gradually, heat gently until thickened but do not boil. Serve round the salmon steaks.

Berry Flower Mould

(Serves 8)
8 ozs gooseberries
6 ozs white sugar
1 lb strawberries, plus 6 large ones to decorate
4 heads of elderflowers
½ pint water
2 pkts gelatine (just under 1 oz in total)

Wash the flower heads and remove any brown petals. Leave three whole and put in a pan with the gooseberries, which have been topped and tailed, enough of the measured water to stop the fruit from burning, and the sugar. Cook gently until the gooseberries are soft. Remove the elderflowers. Purée the gooseberries with the strawberries until completely smooth then sieve to remove any remaining pips. Dissolve the gelatine in the remaining quantity of water, add to the fruit purée. Pour into a wetted mould and leave to set. To serve, invert onto a dish and decorate with the elderflower head on top, and arrange the strawberries sliced between mint leaves around the base.

Strawberry Ice Cream

This is absolutely delicious and compares favourably with the cost of 'boughten' ice cream — but the taste is far superior and worth every minute of its making.

8 ozs ripe strawberries
4 eggs
4 ozs caster sugar
½ pint double cream

Separate the eggs; beat the yolks with the sugar. Whisk the whites until they are stiff and dry. Whisk the cream until it forms soft peaks. Crush the strawberries with a potato masher. Fold the yolks mixture, cream and strawberries into the egg whites carefully until well blended. Pour into a container and freeze to a mushy stage. Beat well to break up the ice crystals and return to the freezer, sealed in a rigid polythene box.

Thaw at room temperature for 8-10 minutes before serving.

Apple Charlotte

Following the association of George III with the Cotswolds, here is a perennial favourite, devised for his wife, Queen Charlotte and named after her. It is best made with a mix of cooking and eating apples.

(Serves 4)
8 ozs prepared weight of Bramley apples
3 ozs butter
8 ozs prepared weight of Cox's eating apples
1 egg
2 tablesps granulated sugar
2 tablesps brown sugar (demerara preferably)
5 slices bread, crusts removed

Cook the apples in a few drops of water, with the sugar, over a low heat until soft. Allow to get cold, beat with a fork and mix in the yolk only of the egg. Set the oven to 200°C (Gas Mark 6). Cut a small disc of greaseproof paper, or baking parchment, to fit the base of a one-pint sized pudding basin, then grease the base and sides thickly with about an ounce of butter. Sprinkle the brown sugar over the butter to coat the inside of the basin. Melt the remaining butter in a pan, cut the bread into fingers and brush the melted butter over each side, line the basin, overlapping where necessary to fill any gaps. Fill with cold apple and make a lid of buttered bread to fit snugly on top as a lid. Cover with an ovenproof plate and a weight. Stand the basin in a baking tray, in case any juice escapes. Bake on the top shelf of the oven for about 40 minutes. Remove the plate and weight and cook for a further 10 minutes to brown the top. Remove from the oven and allow to stand for about 5 minutes before inverting on a serving plate. Serve with cream or custard.

Midsummer Eve's Pudding

This is the eternal favourite summer pudding, made that bit more special by the addition of scented rose petals, but they are optional.

1½ lbs mixed summer fruits: have equal quantities where possible of rhubarb, gooseberries, black or redcurrants and strawberries
8-10 slices of good white bread — get home-baked if at all possible, as the steam baked commercial sliced loaf just goes rubbery
6 tablesps white sugar
2 tablesps fragrant red rose petals (optional)

Prepare the fruit and place in a bowl. Remove the white heels from the rose petals and wash the petals in cold water, tear roughly and add to the fruit. Stir in the sugar, cover and leave to infuse for several hours. Prepare the bread by removing the crusts and cutting each slice into wide fingers. Completely line the base and sides of a 1½ pint sized basin with the bread fingers, pushing together to make sure there are no gaps. Heat the fruit slowly to get the juices running, adding water if necessary, keep the fruit as whole as possible. Spoon the hot fruit and the juice into the lined basin to within about ½ inch of the top. Make a close fitting lid with bread fingers and place a saucer or plate on top to fit snugly to the rim. Weight with a flat iron or a bag of sugar and leave overnight for the juices to seep into the bread and turn it a gloriously ruby red colour. Keep in the refrigerator until a few minutes before needed.

To serve, run a knife carefully round the edge, and you will hear the slurp of the air getting between the basin and the pudding. Place a serving dish on the top, turn upside down, holding the dish firmly against the pudding. It will remain firm until cut. Decorate for a special occasion with a whole rose — or frosted rose petals, and serve with whipped cream sweetened with lavender (just pop a couple of sprigs of lavender in a bowl with the sugar and leave to scent it for a couple of hours, then tip the sugar through a fine sieve to remove the lavender before using), or strained Greek yoghurt.

Sunshine Salad

The golden saffron and orange give this summer salad a lovely sunny look.

(Serves 5-6)
2 cups long grain rice
4 cups water
1 teasp salt
½ pkt saffron strands
3 ozs raisins
6 small jibbols (spring onions)
about 2 fl ozs salad oil
2 ozs flaked almonds
1 tablesp white wine vinegar
fresh parsley
seasoning
1 orange

Cook the rice in the water, as directed on the packet as different types need different cooking times — about 8-10 minutes is usually long enough, with the salt and saffron. Grate the orange rind into a small basin, add the juice, oil, vinegar, seasoning to taste, and whisk vigorously with a fork to thoroughly blend — or you could tip it into a jar, put the lid on firmly and shake. Drain the rice and while it is still hot, add the raisins, chop the onions finely and shred half the almonds — add and stir thoroughly before pouring the dressing over. Scatter the remaining flaked almonds on top and garnish with parsley. Cover and chill before serving.

Farmhouse Omelette

(Serves 4)
1 oz macaroni
1 large or 2 small onions
2 tomatoes, peeled
4 streaky rashers of bacon
1 oz butter
4 eggs
4 tablesps cooked peas
seasoning

Cook the macaroni in a little salted boiling water for about 7 minutes until tender, drain and keep warm while frying the bacon rashers and chopped onion in the bacon fat. The rashers should be crispy, but not overdone, and the onion golden. Whisk the eggs with 2 tablesps cold water and season to taste. Remove the rashers and keep warm. Pour the eggs over the onion in the pan, add the tomatoes, chopped, the macaroni and peas. Cook over a gentle heat until set, cut into quarters to serve, topped with a bacon rasher.

Rose Geranium Sponge

8 ozs butter
8 ozs caster sugar
8 ozs self-raising flour
4 eggs
about 20 small rose geranium leaves, washed and dried
2 tablesps icing sugar

Pre-heat the oven to 190°C (Gas Mark 5). Grease and line two 8-inch sandwich tins. Arrange half the leaves on the lining of the tins. Beat the butter and sugar together until pale and fluffy. Lightly beat the eggs and add a little at a time, adding a spoonful of the flour until well incorporated. Fold in the rest of the flour and divide the mixture between the tins, smoothing the tops but not pressing the air out of the sponge. Bake for 20-25 minutes until golden brown and a skewer comes out clean. Turn on to wire racks to cool, removing the lining paper and leaves. When quite cold, sandwich together with sweet geranium jelly and whipped cream. Place the rest of the leaves on top of the sponge in an attractive pattern. Carefully sift the icing sugar over, quite thickly, and remove the leaves — their shapes clearly left in the sugar.

Snow Rose Cake

(for a special occasion)

Sponge:
4 ozs soft margarine
4 ozs self-raising flour
4 ozs caster sugar
3 egg yolks

Topping:
3 egg whites
2 ozs caster sugar
2 ozs dessicated coconut
a few drops of rose water

Pre-heat the oven to 180°C (Gas Mark 4). Grease an 8-inch sandwich tin. Cream the margarine and sugar together until light and fluffy. Add the egg yolks (lightly broken with a fork) and a spoonful of the flour to prevent it curdling. Fold in the remaining flour and spoon into the tin. Level the top. Whisk the egg whites until stiff and dry. Fold in the caster sugar and coconut and rose water lightly but well blended. Cover the top of the cake completely with this meringue mixture, roughing the top. Bake for 40-45 minutes, covering with a dome of foil if browning. Test with a skewer — it should come out clean when done. The frosted top should be only tinged with gold — like sunshine on snow. Let the cake cool slightly before removing carefully on to a wire tray to finish off. Decorate the top with a cluster of crystallized rose petals, or a whole wild rose.

To crystallize flowers

Crystallized rose petals are so useful and decorative for delicate desserts and cakes, and store well in airtight containers, layered between greaseproof or waxed baking parchment paper. The only roses which successfully crystallize whole are the wild dog roses, so remove the petals of full-blown roses and treat each one separately. Use the old-fashioned sweet smelling roses if you are going to eat them, they are quite delicious.

Wipe each petal with dampened kitchen paper and pinch out the white heel. Beat the white of an egg until it is white and all the opaque liquid has been absorbed. Dip each petal into the egg, shaking off the excess, then draw through a plateful of caster sugar so that each side is coated. Place on paper-lined baking sheets to dry in a cool place.

If crystallizing whole flowers such as primroses and violets — both of which are stunningly simple and delicately flavoured to eat — it is better to paint the egg on to the petals using a small paint brush as the flower will close up when wet and become difficult to sugar evenly. It is also best then to sprinkle the sugar on to the flower rather than draw it through the sugar, for the same reason. The flowers, or petals, should be quite crisp and brittle before using, so need careful handling.

Rose Water

This is quite simple to make if you have sweet-scented roses in your garden, a love of old ways and patience, and makes the basis for delicately flavoured jelly-like sweets, such as Turkish Delight, feather light desserts and memorable whipped cream. As it does not keep for more than a couple of days — being completely free from preservatives — it is useful to freeze any surplus in ice cube trays, then store wrapped in individual squares of foil in a polythene bag. Dried rose petals can also be used, the advantage being that you then need only half the quantity as the flavour and perfume is more concentrated.

Put about 2 lb of freshly picked rose petals in a deep casserole dish, after washing them in running water. Barely cover with water, they will have quite a lot of residue water on them from the washing. Try to use boiled rain water or a filter where possible so that you do not have the chemicals of 'tap water' Cover the dish with a lid and put into a very hot oven until the mixture starts to bubble, reduce the heat immediately and let simmer for a further 10 minutes. Let the liquid get quite cold in the dish, still covered, then strain through a muslin lined sieve into tightly corked bottles. Keep in the refrigerator for two or three days - or freeze until required.

Strawberry Jam

(Makes 3 lbs and a 'taster')
2½ lbs freshly picked and hulled strawberries, small and evenly sized for preference
2 lemons
2¼ lbs granulated or preserving sugar

Spread the prepared strawberries out on an old-fashioned meat dish if you have one, or a large bowl (not metal or enamel). Sprinkle the juice of the lemons over and half the sugar. Leave to steep overnight. Drain the syrupy liquid off the berries into a preserving pan, add the rest of the sugar and bring to the boil rapidly. Continue at boiling point for about 10 minutes. Tip in the strawberries and keep at a steady rolling boil for 15 minutes. Test for set by putting a small blob on a very cold saucer and leaving in a cool place for a few minutes. Push the jam with your finger from the edge to the middle, if it wrinkles then setting point has been reached. Remove the jam from the heat immediately. If not, then boil for a few minutes longer until the next test proves positive. If there is a lot of scum rising on the jam, pop a knob of butter, about the size of a walnut in while it is boiling. Leave the jam to cool to lukewarm before potting in warmed jars, otherwise the fruit will rise. Leave to get quite cold before sealing.

Dairy Cream

This is thick enough to be clotted cream and although it takes a couple of days to make, is well worth the trouble to produce delicious cream in one's own kitchen in the manner of the dairymaids of not so long ago.

4 pints whole milk (Channel Island milk is best because of the higher fat content to start with)

If you have one of those old-fashioned enamel bowls then use it for making cream as it will withstand being heated, if not, then use a flameproof dish, such as Pyrex. Pour in the milk and leave overnight in a cool place for the cream to rise to the surface. It may take a full 24 hours for this. Put over a mere thread of heat to scald. When bubbles rise to the surface ringing the top of the dish, without ever reaching boiling point, remove from the heat carefully and again leave in a cold place to settle — do not put it in the refrigerator either time. After a further 24 hours the crusty surface of cream can be skimmed off with a proper skimmer or a slotted spoon and spooned into a bowl. Then it can be stored in the refrigerator. The skimmed milk left behind can be used as buttermilk for sauces, scones or soups. It is important that the milk is undisturbed as much as possible, so it should be carried with a steady hand at all stages until the cream is skimmed off.

Rose Petal Tea

Use dried petals for this as the flavour is finer. Allow freshly-picked sweet smelling rose petals to dry naturally either in hot sunshine, laying the petals separately on clean cloths, or in the airing cupboard.

Allow 1 tablespoon, just level, not heaped, of dried petals for each cup of tea. Pour boiling water over the petals and leave to infuse for 7 minutes. Strain into wide, delicate china tea cups, or tall, elegant glasses and float two dark red, fresh (washed) petals on top to serve.

Raspberry Wine

This is particularly good because it is ready to drink in about 6 weeks — so can be enjoyed before the summer fades. The quantities rely entirely on the amount of raspberries you have to hand. To make it worthwhile you should aim for at least 3 lbs.

Crush the raspberries thoroughly then sieve to remove the pips. Put into a large pan or crock — earthenware, if possible, after measuring. Boil an equal quantity of water and pour into a jug to get quite cold, then pour it over the fruit pulp left over from the straining. Leave to steep overnight. Strain through muslin onto the juice in the pan or crock. Add 4 tablespoons of white sugar to every pint of juice measured, and stir until every grain has dissolved. Spread a slice of toasted bread with wine yeast (available from large chemists) and place on top to ferment. Cover with a cloth and weight with a board (we used to use the old copper lid). Keep in a cool place for 7 days. Siphon off into wine jar(s), fit the airlock and leave undisturbed for about a month, when the wine should be clear enough to siphon into bottles. It is ready to drink within a week.

Sparkling Strawberry Tea

Mix together equal quantities of well chilled sparkling white wine and iced tea (see below), adding sugar to taste. Dip the edge of each glass in a saucer containing lightly beaten egg white, then into a shallow plate of caster sugar, twirling the glass round to frost the rim evenly. Leave for at least an hour for the frosting to harden. Frost sprigs of mint the same way. Slice three strawberries lengthways and place on top of ice cubes in each glass. Fill to just below the rim and garnish with a sprig of frosted mint.

Iced Tea

This is not hot tea gone cold, but needs to be prepared the day before it is needed. Allow 1 oz of tea to 1 pint of water. Steep the tea (or tea bags) in freshly drawn cold water overnight. Strain and keep covered in the refrigerator until required. To serve, place ice cubes in a tall tea glass, then pour the tea over. Serve with a thin slice of lemon floating on the top.

Cider Tea Punch

1 pint iced tea
2 lemons, washed and sliced
6 cloves
1 pint sweet cider
2 sticks cinnamon
sugar to taste

Pour the tea over the lemons, sugar and spices. Steep for 2 hours. Add the cider. Chill for an hour before serving.

May

above: Curd Cheese (page 42)
left: Quick Cheesecake (page 45)

June

above: Rose geranium Sponge (page 58)
right: Midsummer Eve's Pudding (page 57)

July

above: Rhubarb Syllabub (page 73)
left: Granny's Lemonade (page 76)

August

above: Lemon Honey Loaf (page 82)
right: Rye Bread (page 84)

July

Feasts Long Forgotten Summer Long Remembered

St Swithin's Day, if thou dost rain
For forty days it will remain.
St Swithin's Day, if thou be fair
For forty days, 'twill rain no mair

July was once well-blessed with saints' days on which there was feasting and making merry: the West Country started off by celebrating the martyrdom of Thomas à Beckett on the 7th and in some areas the day is still marked with some kind of sporting occasion; St Swithin's Day on the 15th is remembered in the little verse to foretell the weather for the next forty days; St Margaret, patron saint of safe childbirth, was acknowledged on the 20th and the fisherman saint, St James, on the 25th.

The only true Cotswold feast day to survive into living memory is St Margaret's Day, when the customary dish was Heg Peg Dump, which gave rise to this local ditty:

Nympsfield is a pretty place
Set upon a tump
And all the folks that live there
Eat Heg Peg Dump

The name Heg Peg Dump probably comes from Heg for hedgerow fruits from which the pudding was made, Peg, the pet name for Margaret, and Dump, the dialect word for a boiled pudding. This month's recipes include the famous Heg Peg Dump, a selection using apples, as it has long been a tradition that apples are not ready to eat before St Swithin's Day, and the various uses for the cottage garden rhubarb which has been with us since early spring. It is the first home-grown fruit of the year, and has only been a native plant in our gardens for a couple of hundred years. Often undervalued, rhubarb is so versatile it is worthwhile turning it into drinks, desserts and preserves before it toughens and thickens at the end of the season.

Summer Soup

(Serves 4)
8 ozs prepared strawberries
1 pint good chicken or vegetable stock
1 cucumber, skinned and diced
1 onion
a few leaves of basil
1 small sprig red sage
½ pint double cream
1 oz butter

Gently fry the thinly sliced onion and diced cucumber in the butter until softened, do not allow to brown as it will spoil the colour of the soup. Add the finely-chopped herbs and just under half of the stock, simmer over a low heat until the cucumber and onion are completely cooked. Add the rest of the stock and raise the heat to just boiling point then take off the heat immediately. Allow to cool while making a purée of the strawberries, by sieving or crushing with a potato masher. Mix into the soup and liquidise for a few short bursts. Add the cream and liquidise again until well blended and completely smooth. Serve chilled, decorated with borage flowers.

Severn Salmon Starter

The Severn fishermen have landed some of the best salmon to be found anywhere — so look for local salmon in selected shops in the Cotswolds.

(Serves 4)
12 ozs cooked salmon
1 pkt aspic (crystals)
¾ pint sparkling white wine
1 tablesp finely chopped parsley
1 small cucumber
small bunch watercress

Flake the salmon roughly and arrange in the base of a lightly oiled ring mould. Scatter the chopped parsley over. Dissolve the aspic in ¾ pint hot water, stirring until the crystals have disappeared, then add the wine. Pour into the mould to the top, pouring the rest on a shallow plate. Leave to set. To serve, invert the mould onto a serving dish, loosening the sides with a knife first. Chop the remaining aspic jelly with a wet knife and fill the centre of the ring. Place the washed watercress on the top and arrange thinly sliced cucumber round the edge, overlapping the slices.

Tongue With Raisin Sauce

4-5 lb smoked or pickled tongue
grated rind of 1 lemon
1 bay leaf
l onion
1 clove garlic
1 tablesp white sugar
2 tablesps brown sugar
1 tablesp water
1 teacup beer
4 ozs raisins
1½ tablesps cornflour
2 ozs sliced almonds

Put the tongue, bay leaf, onion — sliced, and garlic in a deep pan with enough water to cover. Bring to the boil, then reduce the heat and simmer steadily for about 3 hours until the tongue is tender. Drain, reserving 2 cupfuls of the stock. Remove the skin and root of the tongue as soon as cool enough to handle.

Put the white sugar and the tablespoon of water in a pan and cook until it caramelizes. Stir in the reserved stock, the beer, brown sugar and raisins. Blend the cornflour with a little water and stir in until well mixed and smooth. Bring to the boil, stirring occasionally. Season to taste. Slice the tongue and heat in the sauce, but do not allow to boil again. Serve, scattered with the almonds and the grated lemon rind.

To Pickle Tongues, Matilda's Way (1868)

First rub them well all over with common salt and let remain for a whole day, then wipe them well with a cloth to get off the slime. Then rub in the ingredients well mixed: 1 lb salt, 2 ozs saltpetre, 2 ozs bay salt, 1½ lb coarse sugar. Let them remain in the pickle for 6 weeks, take them from it when you want to cook, then put them in the water cold.

Chicken And Rice Pot

(Serves 4)
4 large chicken joints
1 onion, peeled and sliced thinly
2 ozs sultanas
2 ozs blanched almonds
1 lemon
1 stick cinnamon
3 bay leaves
8 ozs long grain rice
1 pint chicken or vegatable stock
seasoning
2 fresh peaches

Pre-heat the oven to 180°C (Gas Mark 4). Put the onion in the base of a casserole dish and lay the chicken pieces on top. Sprinkle the sultanas and nuts over. Cut the lemon in wedges and cut out the white central pith and remove pips. Place evenly round the outside of the chicken, together with the cinnamon stick and bay leaves. Spoon the rice to fill in the gaps. Pour over the stock, season to taste, then cover and cook

September

above: Backend Bannuts (Pickled Walnuts) (page 96
left: Bibury Blackberry Pie (page 90)

October

above: Sloe Gin (page 109)
right: Steak and Kidney Pudding (page 100)

November

above: Toffee Apples (page 125)
left: Cotswold Feggy Dump (page 118)

December

above: Golden Christmas Pudding (page 130)
right: Cotswold Lambswool (page 137)

for about 1 hour until the chicken and rice are both cooked. Stir a couple of times during cooking. Skin the peaches and remove the stones. Slice thickly and add to the casserole, cook for a further 15 minutes. Serve with crusty bread. This also makes a good cold dish for a buffet.

Sausage Pudding

(Serves 6)
1½ lbs sausagemeat
3 potatoes, peeled and sliced thin
6 tablesps plain flour
1 teasp baking powder
3 eggs
1 teacup beer
4 fl ozs cream
pinch of chopped thyme
seasoning
about 1 oz lard

Form the sausagemeat into 18 small flat cakes. Brown on both sides in the lard in a frying pan. Lift out onto a plate and fry the potatoes in the remaining fat until just turning brown. Arrange the potatoes in the bottom of a casserole dish and put the sausage cakes on top. Beat the eggs, beer and cream together. Shake in the flour and seasoning and thyme and beat until smooth, pour over the casserole. Bake in a preheated oven at 190°C (Gas Mark 5) for about 30 minutes until cooked through and browned on top. Serve from the casserole.

Heg Peg Dump

Heg is the old word for hedgerow and indicates the wild fruit such as plums from which this 'dump' or pudding, was made.

8 ozs self-raising flour
4 ozs finely shredded suet
1 teasp baking powder
pinch of salt
1 lb plums or damsons
8 ozs cooking apples
6 ozs white sugar
1 tablesp stale sponge cake crumbs

Mix the flour, baking powder, salt and suet together in a bowl and make a soft dough with cold water. Turn out onto a floured board and knead lightly until pliable. Roll the dough out quite thinly and cut off about a third to make the lid. Line a 2-pint greased pudding basin with the rolled out dough, and trim to the edge. Prepare the fruit and remove the stones. Cut the plums or damsons in half and the apples into thinnish slices. Layer in the basin with the sugar and cake crumbs between the fruit. Add about a tablespoonful of cold water. Dampen the edges of the pastry. Roll out the remaining dough and cover without stretching. Press down the edges to seal and trim off excess. Cover with a buttered greaseproof paper and then tie on a white pudding cloth. Steam for 2½-3 hours, or boil in a pan of boiling water, keeping the water topped up with boiling water to come three parts up the side of the basin. Serve from the basin, with thin pouring custard or cream.

Old Fashioned Apple Pupton

4 large cooking apples
about 3 tablesps white wine
3 ozs soft brown sugar
a pinch of powdered cinnamon
1 heaped tablesp stale sponge cake crumbs, finely crumbled
1 oz butter
1 egg yolk

Rough chop the apples, unpeeled, into a pan with just enough wine to thinly cover the bottom of the pan. Stir over a low heat until the apples collapse. Push the apple purée through a sieve and add the sugar while the apple pulp is still hot. Allow to cool slightly before adding the cinnamon and cake crumbs, then later flake in the butter and the lightly forked egg yolk. Turn into a well oiled mould and press down firmly. Chill until needed, then turn out onto a serving dish and decorate — if desired — with cream rosettes and spiked with angelica.

St Swithin's Flaming Apples

(Serves 4)
4 large, juicy and crisp dessert apples
4 ozs raisins and chopped, candied peel, mixed together
4 ozs hazelnuts or almonds, chopped
pinch of grated nutmeg
2 tablesps caster sugar
2 fl ozs water
1 oz butter
4 tablesps brandy

Preheat the oven to 200°C (Gas Mark 6). Wash and core the apples and place in an ovenproof dish. Mix together in a small bowl the raisins, peel, nuts, spice and sugar, then stuff the centre of the apples with the mixture — use a small spoon for this and press it down well so that it is tightly packed. Score round the skin of the apples about a third of the way down. Put the water and butter in the dish and cook on the centre shelf for about 1½ hours, basting the apples with the buttery water about every ½ hour until tender. Remove from the oven, and carefully take off the top rim of skin above the incision — it should peel away quite easily. Warm the brandy, pour over each apple, ignite at the point of serving and bring to the table flaming. Serve with whipped cream.

Rhubarb Syllabub

(Serves 6)
1 lb rhubarb
4 ozs granulated sugar
½ pint double cream
2 medium lemons
3 ozs caster sugar
2 egg whites
1 oz toasted almonds

Prepare the rhubarb and cut into 1-inch pieces. Stew in a pan with 4 tablespoons of water and the granulated sugar for about 10 minutes or until soft, but not stringy and disintegrated. Cool and spoon into a glass serving bowl. Whisk the cream until bulky but not stiff, fold in the grated rind and strained juice of the lemons. Whisk the egg whites until stiff and dry and fold in the caster sugar. Fold the egg mixture through the whipped cream and spoon over the cold rhubarb to cover completely. Decorate with the toasted almonds and serve with shortbread biscuits.

Soured Cream Fish Bake

(Serves 4)
1 lb white fish
1 oz seasoned flour
5 fl ozs soured cream
5 fl ozs mayonnaise
2 spring onions, finely chopped
1 teasp chopped dill
1 teasp lemon juice
2 ozs mature cheese, grated
fresh dill to garnish

Coat the fish in the seasoned flour and place in a greased ovenproof dish. Blend together the cream, mayonnaise, chopped dill, onion and lemon juice. Spoon over the fish so that it is evenly coated. Cover with the grated cheese. Bake in a pre-heated oven at 180°C (Gas Mark 4) for 34-40 minutes until the fish flakes with a fork. Serve hot, garnished with sprigs of fresh dill.

Macaroni Fish Dish

(serves 4)
4 ozs macaroni
½ oz butter
1 onion, chopped
1 oz flour
½ pint milk
5 ozs cheese, grated
8 ozs cooked salmon, or tuna (tinned)
2 small tomatoes
2 tablesps fresh brown breadcrumbs
1 tablesp finely chopped parsley

Cook the macaroni in lightly salted boiling water for about 12 minutes. Drain. Melt butter in a pan and cook the onion until soft but not brown. Blend in the flour and add the milk gradually until smooth. Cook over a moderate heat until the sauce comes to the boil and has thickened. Remove from the heat and add half the cheese, the salmon or tuna, the macaroni and parsley, season to taste and pour into an ovenproof dish. Slice the tomato and lay on the top. Mix the remaining cheese with the breadcrumbs and scatter over. Bake in a pre-heated hot oven for 15 minutes until the cheese and crumbs brown, or grill to toast the top. Serve hot. (This dish also freezes well — without the topping, which can be added when thawed and ready to serve fresh).

Shortbread

4 ozs plain flour
4 ozs butter
2 ozs rice flour
2 ozs caster sugar

Sieve the flour into a basin and mix in the rice flour and sugar. Cut the butter in small pieces and rub into the flour mixture until it is 'crumby' then starts to stick together. Mould firmly to fit a round cake tin, greased and lined, or a shortbread mould. Pinch the edge and prick all over in a pattern. Bake in a pre-heated oven at 170°C (Gas Mark 3) for about 45 minutes until firm and golden. Cool slightly before turning out as it will be very fragile while warm. Dredge the top with caster sugar, leave to get quite cold after marking (while warm) into fingers, which can be cut sharply when the shortbread is cold.

Annie Tinney's Paradise Farm Cakes

2 ozs semolina
3 ozs self-raising flour
3 ozs margarine
1 lemon (or orange)
3 ozs caster sugar
1 egg
2 tablesps icing sugar

Cream the fat and sugar until fluffy, beat in the egg, then stir in the semolina, the sifted flour and the grated rind of the fruit and half the juice. Bake in small cake cases at 180°C (Gas Mark 4) for about 25-30 minutes. When cold, ice with the icing sugar mixed smooth with the remaining fruit juice and allow to set.

Milk Wafers
(Excellent with cheese)

4 ozs self-raising flour
½ oz butter or margarine
about 2 tablesps milk

Sift flour into basin with a pinch of salt (optional). Put the butter or margarine in a small pan with the milk and heat slowly until melted but not hot. Stir into the flour and mix to a smooth paste. Turn onto a floured board and cut into squares, rounds or fancy shapes. Bake on a greased tray at 190°C (Gas Mark 5) for 15-20 minutes until golden brown. Allow to cool slightly before removing from the tray to cool completely on a wire rack. The tops can be sprinkled with coarse sea salt if liked, or a shake of Parmesan cheese, before baking.

Porter Cake

8 ozs butter
8 ozs soft brown sugar
4 eggs (lightly beaten)
10 ozs plain flour
1 level teasp mixed spice
8 ozs raisins
8 ozs sultanas
4 ozs chopped candied peel
2 ozs cherries, chopped
8 tablesps stout or Guinness or strong brown ale

Pre-heat the oven to 170°C (Gas Mark 3). Grease and line a 7-inch cake tin. Cream butter and sugar until light and fluffy. Gradually beat in the eggs, fold in the flour and spice. Add fruit, mix well, then stir in 4 tablespoons of the ale. Spoon into the prepared tin and bake for about 2 hours, covering the top with foil if browning too quickly. Test with a skewer. Allow to cool in the tin for 10 minutes before turning out on a wire tray, upside down. When cold, prick the base all over with a skewer and dribble in the rest of the ale. Allow to seep into the cake before wrapping in greaseproof paper or foil and storing in an airtight tin in a cool place for 6-7 days to mature.

Granny's Lemonade

6 lemons (you can use 4 lemons and 2 oranges for a nice mix)
4 lbs granulated sugar
4 pints water, freshly boiled
1 heaped dessertsp citric acid
1 heaped dessertsp tartaric acid

Wash the fruit well in cold water and mince the whole fruit after removing the pips and cutting into quarters. Completely dissolve the sugar in the very hot water (a plastic bucket is ideal). Allow the water to cool slightly then stir in the acids, followed by the minced fruit. Allow to stand for 36 hours. Strain and bottle. Keep in the refrigerator. It will keep in a cool place for 5-6 weeks, and will freeze very well. Dilute to taste to serve.

Don't throw away the fruit pulp after straining — freeze it in small cartons to use instead of candied peel in cakes and puddings.

Rhubarb Jerkum

This lovely old country wine used to be served on the feast day of St Kenelm, the patron saint of the village church at Minster Lovell, famous for its romantic ruins beside the willow hung Windrush. It is now many years since this home-made wine was served at the charming Olde Swan on St Kenelm's Day.

15 lbs rhubarb
1 gallon boiling water
2½ lbs sugar
1 teasps fresh yeast

Wash, trim and slice the rhubarb. Put into a deep crock and pour the boiling water over. Leave to steep for about 15 minutes then break down with a potato masher. Cover and leave overnight. Strain into a clean bucket and press the rhubarb to extract all the juice, then discard the residue. Stir in the sugar and yeast. Wash the crock and dry thoroughly before returning the wine to it. Cover with a cloth and board and leave to ferment in the usual way before racking and bottling.

Rhubarb Cordial

This looks like a light rosé wine, is very refreshing, cheap to make and non-alcoholic.

2 lbs rhubarb
1 lb granulated sugar
1 large lemon
1 pint water

Wash the rhubarb and cut into l-inch pieces. Put into a saucepan with the sugar. Add the finely grated rind and juice from the lemon and the water. Stir over a low heat to dissolve the sugar, then bring to the boil, reduce the heat and simmer for 20 minutes. Cool, then strain and bottle. Store in the refrigerator for 3-4 days. Serve diluted with soda water.

Home Made Candied Peel

Save lemon, orange and grapefruit skins. Wash them thoroughly, then put in a basin with enough cold water just to cover. Add a generous pinch of salt and soak. Keep covered for two days. Remove the skins and put into a pan with enough fresh water again to cover meanly. Bring to the boil and simmer until the skins are really soft. They should soften in about an hour. Make a syrup by boiling together 2 lb granulated sugar with 2 pints of water until syrupy. Add the drained, cooked skins and boil briskly until the skins look opaque. Lift them out of the syrup onto a large flat dish. Boil the syrup up again and continue to boil until reduced to about half the quantity. Spoon a little of the syrup into the centre of each skin and leave to get quite cold. When really cold and firm, store in dry, well covered jars.

Apple Marmalade

This is a kind of apple butter and is useful to have in the store cupboard as a spread, or as a filling for tarts and cakes.

4 lbs well-flavoured apples
granulated sugar (see below)
16 fl ozs cider
1 teasp ground cloves
½ teasp ground allspice
1 lemon
2 teasps powdered cinnamon

Wash and quarter the apples, but do not peel them or remove the pips. Put into a preserving pan with the cider and bring to the boil quickly. Lower the heat and simmer, uncovered, until the apples are completely collapsed. Cool slightly then rub the fruit and cider mixture through a fine sieve into the washed pan. To every 8 fl ozs of liquid add 4 ozs sugar. Add the spices and the grated rind and juice of the lemon. Stir continuously over a low heat until the sugar has thoroughly dissolved, then raise the heat and boil steadily until the mixture thickens. To test for set put a drop on a cold saucer and leave in a cold place for 3-4 minutes. Push from the edge towards the middle with your finger — if it wrinkles then setting point has been reached, by which time there should be no loose liquid to be seen in the pan. Allow to cool a little then pot in warmed jars while still warm. Seal as for jam.

Rhubarb Chutney

2 lbs rhubarb
2 lbs brown sugar
1 lb sultanas
2 lemons
1 level teasp ground ginger
1 onion, peeled and chopped finely
1 level teasp salt
1 pint malted vinegar
1 level teasp cayenne pepper

Wash the rhubarb and cut into small slices. Grate the rind and add the juice of the lemon to the preserving pan. Add the rest of the ingredients. Bring to the boil, then keep at a steady simmering heat, stirring occasionally, until thickened and brown, with all loose vinegar absorbed. Cool, then pack in warmed jars. Leave to get almost cold before sealing. Leave in a dry cool place to mature for a month before using.

Ploughman's Pickle

2 lbs turnips
1 lb apples
1 lb onions
8 ozs raisins
8 ozs dark brown sugar
1 teasp dry mustard powder
½ oz turmeric
2 shakes of freshly ground pepper
2 ozs salt
2 pints malt vinegar

Peel turnips and cut into very small cubes. Boil in salted water until soft. Drain well. Peel and chop the onions and apples. Mix the turmeric and mustard to a thin paste with the vinegar, add to all other ingredients in a large pan. Bring to the boil and simmer at a slow 'plopping' pace for about an hour, stir often to prevent sticking. Pot and cover while warm. Leave for a couple of weeks to mature before eating.

August

Harvesting and Harvest Home

August takes its name from the Emperor Augustus, who chose to accord his personal seal to the month as it was the one when he gained most fortune. In order that the great Emperor's chosen month should in no way be inferior to the preceding one of July, named after Julius Caesar, the Romans tacked another day onto August. That is why we have two consecutive months of 31 days — the only time it occurs in our calendar. As it is the harvest month, the extra day has been long welcome.

Gathering in the harvest was, until quite recently, the most important time of the year, and everyone was involved. School holidays were fixed by the local clergy in consultation with the landowners of the parish to allow the children to help, and many a Cotswold village school Log Book records: 'School has not opened, on the date previously fixed, as the corn harvest has not yet been gathered in'. The men started work on the farms as dawn broke over the golden cornfields, and the womenfolk cooked meals that could be easily transported in baskets and basins, tied round with snowy white cloths, and the whole family set about the tying and stooking before they could settle down in the shade of the hedgerow to tuck into the home-cooked fare, washed down with home-made drinks kept as cool as possible in stone jars. Toddlers were given their drinks in horn beakers, which only rocked and didn't tip over as easily as the enamel mugs used by their older brothers or sisters. The first day of the month, Lammas Day, was once the important festival of August. Adopted in the Church calendar, it marked the first day of harvest and became known as *Hlafmaesse* in Old English, meaning Loaf Mass, when a specially baked loaf from the first cut of corn was blessed. Harvest Festival is nowadays more likely to be celebrated the next month, but in a good year the whole harvest was safely gathered in during August, to the joy of the workers and relief of the farmers, who showed their gratitude by providing a hearty dinner of roast beef, boiled potatoes, apple pie and plum pudding, a slice of the Harvest Loaf, fashioned like a sheaf of wheat, and good cheese made in the farm dairy, washed down with home-brewed ale and local cider. An old harvest home song gathered from the Warwickshire border sums up the spirit of the times:

Hip! Hip! Hip! for the harvest home
Now we've taken the last load home
I ripped my shirt and I teared my skin
To get my master's harvest in

Local potters fashioned cider jugs in the West Country and examples of the importance of the occasion can be gleaned from surviving jugs and stone jars in country museums, such as:

The potter fashioned me complete
As plainly doth appear
For to supply the harvest men
With good strong English Beer

The Cotswold harvester, well-primed with free beer, might have been brave enough to answer his master's toast with a long Gloucestershire song devised to counter any lecturing on "taking too much" — I am just giving the first and last of the 14 verses:

Dour sarvant, my betters in
station and wealth
And thank'ee fur drinkun the
labourer's health;
And Zur, I cant tell you how
grateful we be
For the good advice thous bin
givun to we.

I 'opes as how these arnest word
I've express'd
Like stwons in a millpond 'oo zinc
in ache breast
Wi' thanks vor thou warnin agin
beer an'pipes;
Thee'st drank we in clarrut —
Yere's to thee in zwipes.

Harvest took up all the month in pre-combine days, so there was little time to celebrate any of the other red letter days which other regions made merry on. Even St Bartholomew's Day on the 24th seems to have passed the Cotsaller by, although no doubt the cottage bee-keepers religiously observed their patron saint in some quiet way of their own — as this was the day it was customary to harvest the honey, and, as this old jingle tells, the hills were once upon a time alive with the soft bleating of sheep and the busy bumble of bees.

Sheep for clover and clover for
bees
Wool and honey from clover leyes
Sheep for wool and wool for
wealth
Bees for honey, and honey for
health
This is what was said of old
On the hills of Cotteswold

Traditional Beer Soup

(Serves 6)
6 cups beer
1 cup sour cream
1 egg yolk
1 dessertsp flour
good pinch salt
dash of cayenne pepper

Beat the egg yolk, flour, seasoning and cream together in a big bowl. Bring the beer to boiling point then remove immediately from the heat. Let it stop seething for a minute then add very gradually to the creamed mixture, stirring all the time to prevent it curdling. Return to the pan and heat through, but do not allow to boil. This is good with garlic toast shapes floated on top sprinkled with grated cheese.

Wolds Chowder

(Serves 4)
1 lb potatoes
3-4 ozs cooked ham, chopped
2 onions
1 pint water
knob of dripping
1 cup single cream
seasoning

Slice the onion and cook in the dripping until just soft, but not brown. Dice the potatoes and add to the pan with the water, bring to the boil, add the ham and reduce the heat. Simmer for about 15 minutes until the potatoes are cooked but not broken. Add the cream and season to taste. Keep at simmering point for 5 minutes before serving.

Cotswold Cheese Soup

(Serves 4)
8 ozs grated Double Gloucester cheese
2 tablesps cornflour
2 onions
1 pint milk and water mixed
½ teasp onion or garlic salt
seasoning
chives or parsley for garnish

Slice the onions thinly and sweat them in the milk and water until soft. Blend the cornflour with a little milk and add to the pan, stirring to prevent lumps. Bring to the boil, reduce heat and cook gently for about 3 minutes. Remove and add the cheese and seasoning, blend well together to allow the cheese to melt, but do not re-heat. Serve immediately garnished with finely chopped parsley or chives.

Harvest Home Brisket

2-3 lbs brisket of beef, boned and rolled
8 ozs bacon pieces
2 onions, sliced
8 ozs carrots, sliced
4 sticks celery, chopped
1 tablesp plain flour
1 tablesp brown sugar
2 bay leaves
6 peppercorns
½ pint beer
1 pint water

Fry the bacon pieces, chopped small, over a low heat to render down the fat. Raise the heat and seal all sides of the beef for a few minutes. Remove, and place in a deep casserole dish with the bacon. Soften, but do not brown the vegetables in the remaining fat. Remove with a slotted spoon and place round the meat. Lower the heat and stir the flour and sugar into the pan with sufficient water to make a thin cream, add beer and the measured water, bring to boiling point, stirring to prevent lumps. Pour over the beef and vegetables. Add bay leaves and peppercorns. Cook in a moderate oven 180°C (Gas Mark 4) for about 3 hours until the beef runs clear juices when pierced. Allow to stand in the liquor until quite cold. It can then be pressed under a plate in a bowl and sliced thinly the following day. Serve with plain potatoes and pickles.

It can, of course, also be served hot with cooked vegetables using some of the liquor poured over the meat. In any case, don't discard the cooking liquid, it makes a very good soup.

Casseroles such as this method of cooking beef, were often finished off in a hay box overnight when the kitchen ranges made small cottages too hot for long cooking. After an hour in the oven, the pot would be fitted in a wooden box or chest which was tightly packed with clean, dry hay. A thick wad of hay was placed on top and the lid of the box firmly strapped over. The pot was kept at simmering point for many hours.

Gloucestershire Hash

(Serves 4)
8 ozs dried haricot or butter beans
2 ozs butter
2 onions, peeled and quartered
4 ozs mushrooms, sliced
1 tablesp flour
8 thin slices of cooked beef or lamb
1 pint good brown stock
1 teasp dried thyme
pinch of dried basil
1 lb ripe tomatoes, quartered
2 teasps sugar
seasoning

Soak the beans in sufficient cold water to cover well, leave overnight. Drain and boil in fresh water for about 30 minutes until tender but not squashy. Melt half the butter and fry the onions until soft, lift out and put in a casserole dish. Fry the mushrooms lightly and add to the onions. Lay the meat slices on top and season to taste. Melt the rest of the butter and stir in the flour adding enough stock to make a smooth paste, then add remainder, stirring to blend until a slightly thickened sauce is formed over a moderate heat. Layer the cooked and drained beans over the meat. Sprinkle with the herbs then pour in the sauce. Finish by layering the tomatoes on top and sprinkle them with the sugar. Cook, uncovered in a pre-heated oven at 180°C (Gas Mark 4) for about 40 minutes. Serve with potatoes, rice or bread and butter.

Plum Pudding

(Serves 4)
1 lb ripe plums, stoned and halved
2 ozs white sugar
3 ozs brown sugar
3 ozs self-raising flour
1 egg, lightly beaten
1 tablesp water
2 ozs butter or margarine

Put the plums in a buttered 1½ pint sized ovenproof deep dish. Spoon over the brown sugar. Beat the butter and white sugar together until light and fluffy. Add the egg and flour alternately, a little at a time, beating well between each addition, then stir in the water. Spoon the sponge mixture on top of the plums, covering them completely. Bake in a pre-heated oven at 180°C (Gas Mark 4) for about 50 minutes until the sponge topping is golden and springy to the touch. Serve hot with custard.

Treacle Tart

This old-fashioned favourite actually uses the refined golden syrup which has been available since the late Victorian age — before that time, the tart was made with treacle or molasses and, of course, that could still be used.

(Serves 4-6)
8 ozs shortcrust pastry
8 tablesps golden syrup
2 tablesps lemon juice
2 ozs fresh white breadcrumbs
pinch of ground ginger

Line a greased shallow pie plate (about 8-inch size) with the rolled out pastry. Trim off the excess from the rim and reserve. Sprinkle the ginger into the breadcrumbs and cover the base evenly. Warm the syrup over a low heat until it is liquid and stir in the lemon juice. Pour evenly over the breadcrumbs. Roll the remaining pastry out and cut into thin strips. Twist slightly and attach to the edges across the tart in a criss-cross lattice pattern. Bake in a preheated oven at 190°C (Gas Mark 5) for 25-30 minutes until the pastry is golden. Serve hot or cold with thick custard.

Dyow Bit

When the Cotsaller's day started at dawn, the stockmen returned home to breakfast at 7 o'clock. Dyow bit is the local pronunciation of Dew Bite — the "bite" to eat that the farm workers had at Dewtide to "stay" them until breakfast time. It is a kind of herby bread pudding, made with whatever herbs could be found in the cottage garden.

4 ozs stale brown bread
about ½ pint milk
4 tablesps minced nuts
1 teasp chopped parsley
a pinch of dried herbs, if fresh are not available
about 1 oz good dripping (or butter)
1 egg

Soak the bread in the milk for half an hour, squeeze until almost dry, catching the milk in a bowl. Break up the soaked bread with a fork and mix in the herbs and nuts. Add the egg to the saved milk and whisk with a fork until blended, then beat into the bread mixture. Spoon into a buttered dish, flake the dripping or butter on top and bake at 180°C (Gas Mark 4), covered with a buttered paper to stop it drying out, for about 1¼ hours until firm, remove the cover and cook for a further 10 minutes to crisp the top. Let get quite cold before cutting into thick wedges to serve with cheese and green salad for a light supper dish or snack.

Cotswold Ham Pudding

(Serves 4)
6 slices, thinly cut white bread
1 oz butter, softened
3 thickly sliced ham slices
3 tomatoes, sliced
3 eggs
1 pint milk

Remove the crusts from the bread and butter the slices. Make 3 sandwiches with the ham and tomato slices, press down with a rolling pin lightly to seal. Cut each sandwich into 4 triangles and place, point sides up, in a buttered, shallow ovenproof dish. Beat the eggs and milk together and season to taste. Strain over the bread triangles, and arrange any tomato slices that are over in the middle of the dish in a line between the triangles. Bake in a preheated oven at 180°C (Gas Mark 4) for 40-45 minutes until the custard has set and the bread crisped. Serve warm.

Lemon Honey Loaf

4 ozs margarine
4 ozs soft brown sugar
1 tablesp honey
1 lemon, grated rind and juice
2 eggs
4 ozs self-raising flour

Beat the margarine and sugar together until light and fluffy. Add the lemon rind and the eggs, lightly beaten, adding a spoonful of the flour to blend smooth, then fold in the rest of the flour. Spoon into a greased and base-lined 2 lb loaf tin. Bake in a pre-heated oven at 180°C (Gas Mark 4) for 35-40 minutes until firm and golden brown. Remove from the oven, but leave in the tin. Put the honey and lemon juice in a small pan and bring to the boil, then pour it over the hot cake in the tin. Allow to get quite cool before turning out carefully to finish off on a cake tray. The lemon syrup topping will sink into the cake as it cools.

Seed Cake

A traditional cake for harvest time, the seed being symbolic of the sowing and harvest cycle. Caraway seed has a very distinct flavour, so it is important not to be too heavy-handed with it when flavouring dishes, but as this recipe is based on the old-fashioned combination of seed and candied peel there is no fruit to counteract the delicate taste of the caraway. It makes an excellent tea-time cake if taken with a cup of tea only, and also as an accompaniment to a glass of sweet wine.

4 ozs butter
4 ozs caster sugar
2 eggs, beaten
6 ozs sifted self-raising flour
1 heaped teasp caraway seeds
1 oz chopped candied peel
1 tablesp warm water

Cream the butter and sugar together until light in colour and texture. Add the egg, a little at a time and beating well. Fold in the flour, caraway and peel, mix until well blended then stir in the water. Spoon into a greased and lined 7-inch cake tin. Sprinkle a few extra seeds on top, if liked, then bake in a pre-heated oven at 180°C (Gas Mark 4) for about 1 hour until a skewer comes out clean and the cake nicely browned. Cool on a wire tray.

Cotswold Lardy Cake

The lardy cake is a speciality of Gloucestershire and its neighbouring county, Wiltshire — both pig-rearing regions with plenty of good white lard with which to cook good old-fashioned dishes. Once, the lardy cake was as traditional as seed cake and apple pie for celebrating harvest home. It was then called the countryman's fruit breadcake — being made of an enriched bread dough and layered with fruit to make a cake.

For the basic dough:
8 ozs strong white flour
½ teasp salt
½ oz white pure lard
1 oz white sugar
½ oz fresh yeast
¼ pint warm milk

For the filling:
4 ozs currants
2 ozs sultanas
2 ozs best white lard
2 ozs soft brown sugar
½ teasp mixed spice

Topping:
1 egg, beaten
2 ozs granulated sugar

Make the dough by sifting the flour and salt in a bowl, rub in the lard and make a well in the centre. Blend the yeast and sugar together in a jug until it creams by adding 2 tablespoons of the warm milk. Mix in the rest of the milk and pour into the well. Draw the flour in from the sides until a smooth dough is formed. Mould into a ball shape and leave in a greased bowl, and cover with greased polythene, to rise in a warm place for 30 minutes, when it should be doubled in size. Roll out lightly on a floured board to an oblong shape. Dot half the lard over the dough, then spread it evenly, sprinkle on half the sugar, spice and fruit, fold over the bottom to a third of its length, then bring the top third over. Seal the edges lightly by pressing with a rolling pin. Roll out again, lightly and repeat the layering process. Place in a well-greased baking tin with the seal underneath. Put to rise again under greased polythene, in a warm place for 45 minutes. Pre-heat the oven to 200°C (Gas Mark 6). After the dough has proved again, brush the top with the egg and sprinkle the sugar over. Bake for 30-35 minutes, taking care to cover the top if the glaze starts to burn. Take care when turning out of the tin to cool as the syrupy topping will be hot and will drip. When cooled, the topping will have formed a toffee-like crust. Eat cold, or warmed, the day of baking.

Lammas Loaf

This is a very good milk bread recipe which gives a pliable dough suitable for plaiting in a traditional 'ears of wheat' shape to represent harvest and scattered with seeds to symbolise the growing cycle. It will also make excellent cottage loaf shapes.

(For one good sized loaf)
1 lb strong white flour
1 oz fresh yeast
1 level teasp salt
1 level teasp sugar
½ pint warm milk
1 egg and a little milk to glaze

Make the dough as for Lardy cake (previous recipe) and leave to rise for 45 minutes. Turn onto a floured board and 'knock back' — kneading the air bubbles out of the dough — then reshape into a ball and put again to rise, covered as before, for a further 15 minutes. Knead or shape, or plait the dough in whatever form you wish it to be — a cottage loaf has a base of two-thirds moulded into a round, with the remaining dough moulded into a ball to sit on top. Seal top to bottom by pressing a floured end of a wooden spoon right through the top to about an inch into the base. After shaping leave for a further 15 minutes to rise again before baking in a pre-heated oven at 220°C (Gas Mark 7) for 30-35 minutes. The top can be brushed with egg and milk and scattered with poppy seeds, or dusted with flour and left plain. It can be baked on a greased tray, in a tin or in a well greased, clean flower pot of clay. To test if done, bread should sound hollow when the bottom is knocked with your knuckles. Leave to cool on a wire tray.

Rye Bread

This was the coarse bread which sustained generations of farmworkers until wheat flour became more affordable. Today, as with many peasant foods, rye bread has a status value for its nutritional and fulsome advantages over factory made bread.

(Makes 1 large and 1 small loaf)
14 ozs strong white flour
14 ozs rye flour or meal
pinch of caraway seed
3 level teasps salt
1 flat dessertsp brown sugar
1 teasp black treacle
16 fl ozs warm water
¾ oz fresh yeast

Mix the flours, salt and caraway together in a bowl. Blend the sugar and yeast together with the treacle and continue as for Lammas Loaf (page 71).

A lighter loaf can be made by replacing the sugar and treacle with 1 tablespoon honey and omitting the caraway seeds.

Harvest Drinks

In my Gran's old notebook marking the place for drinks for harvest-time, was a faded newspaper cutting dated 1890 advertising the success the Total Abstinence Society was having in the Cotswolds over the *topers and totalers*. With concerts in village halls, where hitherto imbibers revealed their former vices with harvest ale, were advertisements for their specially blended tea, priced at £l.ls.8d. per 10 lb chest including rail carriage.

The following recipes were extracted from the church monthly.

Stokos

Mix 6 ozs of fresh oatmeal, ground as fine as flour, with water to a thick creamy substance. Add 6 ozs sugar and one thinly sliced lemon. Add a gallon of boiling water, while stirring thoroughly. Cost: 1 shilling for 5 gallons.

Cokos

Mix 4 ozs freshly ground oatmeal, 4 ozs cocoa and 6 ozs sugar with a little water. Add a gallon of boiling water, stirring the while. Take to the fields in a stone jar. Cost: 4d per gallon.

Hopkos

Boil ½ oz of hops and ½ oz of bruised root ginger in 1½ gallons of water for 25 minutes. Add 1 lb of best brown sugar and boil for a further 10 minutes. Strain into a cask while still hot. Store in a cold cellar or corner of the larder.

Gran's addition read: dried horehound may be used instead of hops as this costs 3d per gallon.

Gramp's sturdy handwritten note, in indelible pencil read: Proper harvest ale can be brewed from Cotswold barley for £l per 100 gallons!

Ginger Beer

A traditional harvest time brew, non-alcoholic, and ready to drink in 3 days, ginger beer has the advantage of being an all the year round drink, quite independent of seasonal fruits or vegetables in its making. I remember my Granny making it by the gallon, but always with a mysterious sounding 'mother' in it — a kind of fungus which was saved from one batch to start off another, rather like the culture needed for making yoghurt. However, this recipe is quite successful without the 'mother'.

(Makes about 8 pints)
1 oz root ginger
1 lb granulated sugar
1 oz cream of tartar
1 lemon, scrubbed
8 pints boiling water
1 oz baker's (or wine) yeast

Put the ginger in a scrap of cloth and bruise it by hitting with a hammer — this releases the full flavour. Thinly pare the rind from the lemon and squeeze out the juice. Put the bruised ginger, cream of tartar and lemon rind in a clean plastic bucket and pour on the boiling water. Add the lemon juice and stir with a long-handled wooden spoon. Cool to about blood heat then add the yeast which has been creamed with a little water. Cover with a weighted cloth and leave in a warm place for 24 hours. Skim off the froth and using a jug to 'bale out' the beer, fill strong bottles with corks which can be tied down with string or florists wire. Do not tie too tightly — leave a little play on the tie. Store in a cool place for 3 days, examining quite often. If the fermentation seems too lively, then release a bit of pressure by loosening the ties on the corks slightly. The ginger beer is ready to drink as soon as fermentation stops.

Pickled Eggs

Another excellent accompaniment to the good old-fashioned bread and cheese supper is pickled eggs, once a firm favourite in the village pub fare in the days when it was quite usual for the carters and ploughmen to call in at the local on their way home, and eat their own bread and cheese (if they had any left from their day in the fields). Home-pickled fresh eggs are extremely simple to prepare and make an ideal store food which improves with keeping. The small round bantam eggs are particularly good.

To pickle a dozen — the traditional Cotswold hens still lay their eggs in dozens, they are refreshingly non-metric in their production!

1 dozen fresh-laid eggs
2 blades of mace
about a pint of good spiced or white vinegar

Hard-boil the eggs for 12 minutes, moving them gently in the water within the first few minutes to centralise the yolks. Drain and tip into a bowl under the tap and run cold water on them immediately. This prevents a black ring from forming round the yolks. When cool enough to handle, shell the eggs and pack into clean dry jars, add a blade of mace to each jar and cover with vinegar. Seal completely airtight and leave in a dark place to mature for at least a month before eating.

September

Feast and Fairings, Mops and Michaelmas and Clippings — with Pig's Face, Puppy Dog and The Devil's Nutting Bag

September is a festive month. Avening Feast celebrates the patronage of its Church of the Holy Cross with Pig Face sandwiches, in honour of the time when Queen Matilda, wife of William the Conqueror, feasted with the builders of the church at its completion. Many people still refer to the custom as Pig Face Day. It is believed that the date of the royal feast was September 14, 1080, which makes it one of the most endurable of our many traditions.

Ancient hiring fairs, known as Mops, have lost their original purpose of being a kind of open-air employment exchange. Well into living memory, it was the time when farmworkers and domestic servants went to the Mop to offer themselves for hire. Each wore a token of their calling: the carter had a length of whipcord round his hat; the shepherds pinned a lock of fleece to their smocks and the girls dressed up in their best clothes. The only contract of service was the payment of one shilling to bind the servant for a year, but the third consecutive hiring fair was known as the Runaway Mop — this was an opting out time for the hired servant to get out of the deal.

The scene is graphically illustrated in these selected verses from an old folk song:

We aal be gwain to Cizzeter Mop
On Monday marn so jolly
Along wi' Bill an' Carter Joe
An' Lizer Jane and Molly
We aa1 turn's out in clane white smocks
An' billycocks so grand
An' Joe he twisted whip cord
Aal round him vor a band
Thur wur gurt big blue and yeller vlowers
On top o' Lizer 's 'at
An' Bill drawed out in karderoys
Red Hankurnchief an' that
The volks did stare as we wur gwain
An' many 'ollered out —
"Go and get hir 'd at Cizzeter Mop
Ya gurt lumbrin' country lout"
We walk'd aal droo the noisy Mop
A 'an Bill and Molly
An' seed the wenches stan' for hire
In aal thur fol-de-rolly
An' thur wur Cerney men an' bwoys
Wi'girls from Ashun Kayns
An' Barnsley volks cum ridin' in
A wagin wi'out reins

Several more verses describe the attractions of Punch and Judy, wrestling booths and peep-shows.

We went into the Dree Kauks Inn
An' had a pint of ale
An' call'd to zee the Old Blak Hoss
The King's Arms an' The Bell
An' furder down twur zinging zongs
'Bout wiskee, gin an' rum
Thay axed I to buy a ditty then
'bout the Harvest Whoam

The Harvest Home ditties were equally as long, each chorus toasting the health of the master, the mistress, and all the members of their household in turn — no doubt to spin out the times to refill the cup, as this chorus suggests:

Here's health to the man this house do belong
For providing of us this good cheer
Here's health to his wife all the days of her life
Lord send him good crops for next year

And prosper his flock, and all his whole stock
His family well to maintain
Then take up this cup and drink it all up
For there's plenty to fill it again

Before Michaelmas on the 29th, the Feast of St Michael, on which settling up of rents and dues and the year's hiring terminated, Nutting Day on the 3rd was a traditional holiday from school to gather nuts from the local woods. The village schools on the edges of Cirencester Park maintained the custom until just before the last war. Coates School records speak of 'the day Lord Bathurst opens his woods for nutting'.

Nuts are supposed to be at their perfection on the 3rd of September, but avoided at all costs on the 21st, for this is The Devil's Nutting Day. An old Cotswold expression is "as hard as the Devil's nutting bag".

A colourful festival which has survived the years, is the Clipping Ceremony at Painswick. Clipping in this case has nothing to do with trimming the legendary 99 yews in the churchyard, or the shearing of sheep — as often surmised, but comes from the Saxon *ycleping*, meaning embracing. On the Sunday of, or immediately following the 19th September, the parishioners encircle their parish church of St Mary for the ceremony, joining hands they surge towards the church while singing the Clipping hymn: 'Daily, daily sing the praises'. Flowers are worn in pretty garlands by the girls and buttonholes by the boys, and even the pet dog has been seen to sport a floral collar. At the end of the service every child is presented with a Clipping Bun — a large extra fruity and spicy bun made at Walklett's Bakery — Mrs Enid Walklett, in whose family the bakery has been for about 120 years, says that each year some 350 buns are made for the children, with a further 50 for the band tea afterwards. As well as the bun, the children receive a shilling (now a 5p coin).

To find the origin of the legendary 'Puppy Dog Pie', I discovered from another local lady, Mrs Peggy Perrin, that the tale told to her by her father, who had it from his grandfather — in the delightful way that Beatrix Potter heard of the Tailor of Gloucester — that the Painswick lads many years ago had a long-standing feud with the lads of neighbouring Whitehill. Every Saturday night they had a right rough and tumble on the hill, then one night the Painswick boys called a truce and as a token of their intent to keep the peace with their neighbours, invited their adversaries to a feast the following week. The Whitehill boys accepted and enjoyed a feast of meat pies specially prepared for them, only to be told afterwards by their hosts that they had eaten the dogs of Painswick.

For ever after, and even now by the native Painswickians, a locally-born man is known as Painswick Bow Wow. It's a tale which has been nurtured through the ages because Puppy Dog Pie became a traditional dish served at family gatherings at Painswick Feast — the Sunday of the Clipping Ceremony — but the pies were of apple, with a pie funnel of china shaped like a small dog. Mrs Perrin, who kept the newsagents in Painswick for many years, recalls selling the specially made Painswick Pie funnels.

Country Liver Paté

12 ozs liver — chicken, pig, or turkey, as preferred
1 oz butter
4 ozs streaky bacon
1 egg
1 small onion, grated
½ pint milk
1 clove garlic, crushed
1 oz plain flour
1 bay leaf
seasoning

Mince the liver and bacon together. Once is enough if you want a coarse textured paté, if you prefer it creamy smooth then you will need to mince again, or even liquidise it. Make a white sauce by blending the butter, melted with flour and adding the milk. Bring to boiling point, stirring to prevent lumps, then simmer to cook the flour for a couple of minutes. Remove from the heat and stir in the egg. Mix together with the liver and stir in the onion and garlic.

Spoon into a buttered shallow dish and put the bay leaf on top. Place the dish inside a covered casserole dish with enough water in it to come half way up the side of the liver dish. Cook for about 1 hour in a pre-heated oven at 180°C (Gas Mark 4), or until firm. Leave to cool. Cover with foil or cling film and, preferably, leave in a cool place for 24 hours for the flavours to mingle. Serve with toast fingers or crusty bread and a small salad as a starter.

Fork Fish Starter

(Serves 4)
2 eggs, hardboiled
1 stick celery, prepared
6 ozs salmon, or tuna fish, flaked
1 small onion, chopped very fine
2 tablesps mayonnaise
about 24 grapes
small sprigs of parsley for garnish

Serve in scallop shells if you have them, or in small flat dishes. Divide the flaked fish between the dishes. Finely chop the celery and scatter over the fish, then the onion. Dribble the mayonnaise over to cover very thinly. Slice the eggs and lay the slices down the centre of each dish. Halve and de-pip the grapes and lay on top in a decorative pattern. Garnish with tiny sprigs of parsley. Cover with cling film and chill for at least an hour. This light starter can be eaten with just a fork.

Country Style Pork and Baked Beans

Home made baked beans bear little resemblance to the ubiquitous canned version in its over-sweet runny sauce, which has found its way into our national diet. The dish of pork and beans is, in fact, very old peasant fare — yet good enough, it is said, to have been favoured by George III. We seem to have adopted the New World version of the baked bean to the detriment of keeping faith with our own culinary invention — for it was from England that the Pilgrim Fathers took the recipe across the Atlantic.

It is just the dish to cook in farmhouse ranges, or a slow cooker as it does take time — but, well worth the trouble.

(Serves 6-8)
1 lb fresh pork, as lean as possible, cut into small cubes
2 rashers streaky bacon, chopped
1 lb haricot beans
2 ozs butter
1 lb tomatoes, skinned
1 flat teasp salt
½ teasp freshly ground pepper
¼ teasp dried basil
¼ teasp dried thyme
1 level dessertsp sugar
1 pint good stock, brought to the boil

Soak the beans overnight in just enough cold water to cover. Fry the pork in the butter until just lightly browned all over, then add the bacon pieces and fry for a few minutes until the fat runs, remove with a slotted spoon. Put the drained beans in a deep, buttered, casserole dish just enough to cover the bottom. Put the pork and bacon on top, then the remaining beans. Sieve, or liquidise, the tomatoes and mix in the herbs and the hot stock, seasoning to taste. Pour over the pork and beans. Cover with a close fitting lid, or foil. Cook in a pre-heated oven at 150°C (Gas Mark 2) for 4-5 hours. The dish can be re-heated thoroughly if made in advance.

Michaelmas Goose

Whoever eats goose on Michaelmas Day
Shall never lack money for his debts to pay

This traditional old song dates back to the time when the tenants paid their dues to the landlords, and a goose fattened on the common leazing lands at Michaelmas, the third quarter day of the year. Michaelmas goose is less fatty than at Christmas, so it makes a very good meal, especially when stuffed with rich sausagemeat and prunes, as in the Middle Ages. For a less rich stuffing, combine chopped apples and walnuts with breadcrumbs.

1 goose, prepared and wiped with a damp cloth
6 ozs prunes, leave the stones in initially
about ½ pint wine, red or white
8 ozs sausagemeat
1 egg yolk
¼ teasp ground ginger
¼ teasp grated nutmeg
¼ teasp ground cinnamon
1 tablesp chopped parsley
seasoning

Wash the prunes and leave to soak in the wine overnight to 'plim up'. Place in a pan with their wine, adding a little more to cover the prunes if necessary, and bring to the boil. Simmer gently for about 20 minutes until they are soft. Drain and reserve the liquid. Remove the stones from the prunes and chop finely. Tip into a mixing bowl with the sausagemeat, spices and parsley, season and stir in enough of the liquid to make a soft but not sloppy mixture. Bind with the egg yolk and fill the cavity of the bird, pressing the stuffing well in. Secure the end. Place the stuffed bird in a roasting tin and prick the skin all over with a skewer, then rub all over with salt. Roast at 180°C (Gas Mark 4) for an initial 15 minutes, then calculate the cooking time at 15 minutes per pound weight of dressed goose. Drain off the fat as it runs during the cooking, but it will not need basting. Let it rest for 20 minutes in a warm place before carving.

Painswick Puppy-Dog Pie

No! Don't let the title put you off, the only dog that was ever in the Painswick Pie in living memory was the little dog-shaped pie funnel. This is an apple pie, just like every Mother made. It was traditional to have this on Clipping Sunday at family gatherings. Apple pie has been with us for a very long time, as borne out in the maxim "As English as apple pie"; and it even moved a poet of the early 18th century to break into verse praising this most loved British pudding.

Of all the delicates that Britons try
To please the palate and delight the eye,
Of all the sev'ral kinds of sumptuous fare
There is none that can with apple pie compare

(Serves 6-8)

1½ lbs apples, mixed cooking and eating make a good mix but use slightly more of the cookers than eaters
8 ozs shortcrust pastry
4 ozs granulated sugar
grated rind of 1 lemon
6 cloves
1 tablesp caster sugar

Prepare the apples and slice them together. Mix the granulated sugar and lemon rind together in a small bowl. Layer the apples in the bottom of a 1½ pint sized pie dish and put a china pie funnel in the centre. Sprinkle the sugar mix over, then layer with apples again and finish with the rest of the sugar mix. Put the cloves evenly between the layers. Roll out the pastry and cut off a thin strip. Grease the edge of the dish and press the pastry strip round. Dampen it with water and place the pastry top over, pressing the edges down firmly with a floured fork. Make a small hole in the top to allow the steam to escape. Brush the top with cold water and scatter the caster sugar over evenly to give a nice crisp crust. Bake in a pre-heated oven at 200°C (Gas Mark 6) for 20 minutes then reduce the heat to 190°C (Gas Mark 5) to cook for a further 20 minutes, when the apples should be cooked through and the pastry golden brown. Serve hot or cold with custard or cream.

Blackberry and apple pie is made in the same way, substituting some of the weight of apples with blackberries.

Bibury Blackberry Pie

12 ozs shortcrust pastry made with all lard
1 lb ripe blackberries
4 ozs soft brown sugar
½ teasp grated nutmeg
2 ozs butter
2 tablesps sherry

Layer the blackberries on a flat dish and sprinkle the brown sugar over. Leave to steep for several hours until the juice starts to run. Line a greased pie dish with half the pastry, not too thinly rolled. With two spoons scoop up the blackberries, draining the juice from them back into the flat dish, and layer the fruit in the pastry case. Flake half the butter over the berries, then finish with another layer of fruit, again flake the butter over. Put the juice in a small pan with the sherry and warm together but do not boil. Cool slightly then spoon carefully over the fruit taking care not to wash the butter away. Cover with a top of pastry, again not too thinly rolled. Make a slit in the top and brush with milk to glaze. Bake at 190°C (Gas Mark 5) for about 45 minutes until the pastry is golden brown and the berries are tender. Serve hot with thin pouring custard or cream.

Pig's Face Brawn

The pig's face feast which was a tradition in the Stroud valley village of Avening for centuries, ended up as brawn sandwiches served at the local pub. It is now only revived occasionally. This recipe is based on a very old one in which my Gran wrote "it is best to use your own feet than those of the butcher's" — she obviously meant that the family pig's trotters were superior to "boughten". But that was all in the days when every cottage had its own pig in the sty and every scrap of it was used "except the squeak". This brawn is very good as a snack with salad or in sandwiches.

½ pig's head, cut into 4 pieces, the butcher might chop it for you
2 trotters
2 onions
3 sprigs of fresh parsley
2 carrots
2 bay leaves
6 peppercorns
6 cloves

Wash the head and trotters thoroughly — although nowadays they will be sold cleaned. Put to soak with a good handful of salt in a big bowl of cold water. Leave overnight, then drain and wash again. Put into a large saucepan and cover with cold water. Bring to the boil and skim off any scum which may have risen. Now add the prepared and chopped vegetables and spices. Cover the pan and keep simmering for about 2½ hours until the meat is cooked. Remove the head and trotters and cut off all the meat from them, discarding any gristle, and put into a bowl. Return the bones to the pan, but discard any skin. Add 1 teaspoon of salt and boil the stock rapidly until it is reduced down to about 1 pint. Strain into a jug, leave to get almost cold when any fat can be skimmed off the top. Chop the parsley finely and mix in with the meat pieces, then add the cooled, skimmed liquid. Season to taste and pack into a pudding basin to set completely.

Liver and Onions

Pig's liver has a stronger flavour than the milder and softer calves' or lambs' liver, but either can be used.

(Serves 4)
1 lb liver, washed and trimmed of any tubes, sliced thinly
4 rashers of bacon, roughly chopped
½ pint beef stock
2 large onions, sliced
1 oz good dripping
1 oz flour
2 level teasps salt
shake of black pepper

Fry the bacon in the dripping until the fat changes from white to opaque, but do not crisp up. Remove from the pan and keep warm. Fry the onions in the remaining fat until they start browning a little. Stir in the flour to make a smooth paste and cook for 1 minute, stirring all the time. Gradually add the stock and seasoning. Stir frequently to keep the sauce smooth and bring to boiling point. Add the liver and the bacon. Cover the pan and reduce the heat to a simmer. Cook for about 15 minutes until the liver is tender — serve with mashed potato and buttered cabbage for a main meal or with thin toast fingers as a snack or supper dish.

Nut and Orange Cake

This is a good light cake, as an alternative to rich fruit cake — plain, it is a good cut-and-come-again type; decorated with marzipan fruits, it makes a good centrepiece to parish harvest festival suppers, which are increasingly popular in the Cotswold villages.

6 ozs soft margarine
5 ozs light, soft brown sugar
3 eggs, lightly beaten
4 ozs self-raising flour, sieved
4 ozs wholemeal self-raising flour, sieved
8 ozs hazelnuts, toasted then crushed
1½ teasps ground mixed spice
1½ teasps baking powder
grated rind of 2 oranges and the juice of 3

Beat the margarine and sugar together until light and fluffy. Add the eggs a little at a time and beat well between. Fold in the flours and spice and baking powder, previously sieved together to blend evenly. Stir in the orange rind and juice and the nuts. Spoon into a greased and base lined 7-inch cake tin, smoothing the top, and bake in a pre-heated oven at 180°C (Gas Mark 4) for about 1¼ hours, until a skewer comes out clean. Remove from the oven and let cool in the tin for 20 minutes before turning out to finish on a wire rack as the cake is very light.

If you want to decorate it for a special occasion, brush the top, when completely cold, with 4 tablespoons of sieved and warmed apricot jam. Decorate with marzipan leaves round the outer edge and fashion an assortment of marzipan fruits to fill the centre.

Revel Buns

This is a very old recipe for very rich buns made specially for village revels. This was in the days when cream from the dairy was more a feature of everyday cooking — cream, like saffron, is decidedly more expensive today, but for a special occasion it is nice to make a luxury old-time slice of the fare our forefathers enjoyed at their festivals.

1 lb plain flour
2 teasps salt
2-3 tablesps saffron milk
1 dessertsp sugar
1 egg
6 ozs currants
2 ozs best white lard or butter
pinch cinnamon
½ oz fresh yeast
5 fl ozs double cream
handful of washed sycamore leaves

To make the saffron milk, dissolve a few strands of saffron in the milk and leave to steep overnight. Sift the flour and salt into a mixing bowl together with the cinnamon. Cream the yeast with the sugar in a small bowl. Heat the saffron milk with the fat just to melt it, then add, with the yeast mix, to the flour. Stir in the beaten egg with the cream and mix to a smooth dough. Knead well and put to rise in a greased bowl, covered with greased polythene, until doubled in size. Knock back on a floured board and sprinkle with the currants. Knead the currants well into the dough, then cut into even sized pieces. Shape between floured hands into neat buns. Put to rise again for 30 minutes. Have ready the washed and well-dried sycamore leaves. After the last proving, wrap the buns carefully in the leaves and place, join side down, on a baking tray. Bake in a pre-heated oven at 190°C (Gas Mark 5) for about 35 minutes. Unwrap as soon as cooked and cool the buns on a wire tray.

Clipping Buns

The Painswick buns, made to distribute to the children after the Clipping Ceremony, and for the band tea, are about as big as a Hot Cross Bun, but more fruity and spicy. Some 400 Clipping Buns are made every year by Walklett's Bakery as has been the custom for well over a century. The following recipe for currant buns makes a kind of teacake texture, which is also very good toasted when the buns are a day or two old.

1 lb plain flour
pinch of salt
½ oz fresh yeast
2 ozs butter
3 tablesps milk, lukewarm
6 ozs currants
¼ teasp ground cinnamon
¼ teasp mixed spice
3 ozs caster sugar
Glaze: **2 tablesps granulated sugar**

Sift the flour, salt and spices together in a bowl. Cut the butter into small pieces and rub in until it resembles breadcrumbs. Cream the yeast with the sugar and milk and leave for about 10 minutes when it should be frothy on top. Make a well in the middle of the flour and pour in the yeast mixture. Bring in the flour from the edges and mix to a stiff dough. Place in a greased bowl, cover with greased polythene, or a floured cloth, and leave in a warm place to prove for an hour. Scatter the currants over the dough and knead on a floured board. Cut the dough into evenly sized pieces and shape into round buns. Place on a well buttered baking tray and leave to rise, covered again, in a warm place for a further 30 minutes. Dissolve the granulated sugar in a tablespoon or two of tepid water and brush the tops evenly to glaze. Bake in a preheated oven at 220°C (Gas Mark 7) for 15-20 minutes until golden brown and hollow sounding when the bottom is tapped with the knuckles. Leave to cool on a wire tray.

Fairings

These ginger biscuits were a traditional part of the Hiring Fairs, or Mops as they are called in the Cotswolds.

4 ozs plain flour
pinch of salt
1 level teasp baking powder
1 level teasp bicarbonate of soda
3 tablesps golden syrup
½ level teasp mixed spice
1 level teasp ground ginger
2 ozs butter

Sift the flour with the salt, baking powder and bicarbonate of soda into a bowl. Stir in the spices. Rub in the butter, then add the sugar. Warm the syrup until it is liquid enough to pour, then mix into the dry ingredients, blending well to form a fairly stiff mixture. Take a spoonful at a time and shape into small balls. Place about 4 inches apart on well-buttered trays and flatten with the back of a fork slightly. Bake in a pre-heated oven at 200°C (Gas Mark 6) for 7-8 minutes until golden brown. Leave to cool slightly before removing with a fish slice onto a wire tray to harden off. Store in an airtight tin.

Old-Fashioned Gingerbread

The gingerbread stall was as much a part of the old Hiring Fairs as the servants lined up offering their services to employers.

8 ozs self-raising flour
3 ozs granulated sugar
1½ level teasps ground ginger
pinch of salt
4 ozs margarine
2 teasps golden syrup
4 ozs mixed, or candied peel, chopped finely
2 egg yolks, beaten

For the topping:
egg white
2 tablesps granulated sugar

Put the flour, salt, sugar and ginger in a bowl and stir together. Melt the margarine in a small pan with the syrup until runny, but not oily. Remove from the heat and stir in the egg yolks. Tip into the dry ingredients and beat well. Tip about half of the mixture into a greased oblong tin measuring about 7 x 4 inches. Press into the corners.

Scatter the peel over evenly then cover with the rest of the gingerbread. Brush the lightly forked egg white over the top quite thickly, then sprinkle the granulated sugar over. Bake in a preheated oven at 170°C (Gas Mark 3) for about 30 minutes, turning the tin round and covering if browning unevenly. Remove from the oven and mark into squares while warm, ready to cut cleanly when cold.

Treacle Toffee

This old-time favourite of the sweet stalls at fairs and markets used to be known as 'stickjaw' by the children. Toffee goes sticky when exposed to the air, so keep wrapped.

(Makes about 1½ lb)
4 ozs unsalted butter
8 ozs black treacle
1 tablesp white vinegar
1 lb light soft brown sugar
2 tablesps water

Put the butter in a pan with the vinegar and water and heat gently until the butter has melted. Stir in the sugar and treacle. When every grain of sugar has dissolved while stirring to keep the sides well scraped down into the pan, bring to the boil — the temperature on a gauge should be 138°C (280°F). Remove the pan from the heat to let the bubbles subside before pouring the toffee into a well-oiled square tin to set. While it is setting, mark into squares several times — as it tends to glug back over the marks — this makes it easier to break into pieces when quite cold. Wrap each piece in cling film or cellophane paper and store in an airtight jar or tin.

Barley Sugar Twists

These fairground sweets still retain their original name from the barley from which they were first flavoured — it has been the custom 'south of the border' to use lemon rather than barley. If, however, you want to try barley flavouring, blanch about 2 ozs barley kernels in scalding water, then strain and run cold water through to cleanse it first. Boil until tender in about ¾ pint water, with a thin paring of lemon peel, then strain a couple of times through a muslin lined sieve and use instead of the water in this recipe.

(Makes about 3 dozen twists)
12 sugar cubes
1 lemon, washed
1 lb granulated sugar
½ pint water
pinch of cream of tartar
yellow food colouring

Rub the cubed sugar over the lemon to extract the zesty oil in the skin; place with the granulated sugar and water in a pan and dissolve the sugar over a low heat. Add the cream of tartar and raise to boiling point 118°C (245°F) on a sugar thermometer. Add the juice of the lemon and raise the heat a little. Remove the pan from the heat and stir in about 5 drops of food colouring, if liked. When it has stopped bubbling, pour the mixture into an oiled shallow pan of a swiss roll shape. Mark with an oiled knife after about 5 minutes into narrow strips. Then, with the tin over a warmstove to keep the mixture pliable, pull the strips from the tin and cut each in half with oiled scissors. Twist quickly and let harden off on an oiled tray. Keep stored in waxed paper or cling film, standing upright in a tall glass jar. These barleysugar twists freeze successfully, just pack the wrapped twists in a polythene bag —storage time two months, thaw for an hour before eating.

Backend Bannuts

These are pickled walnuts, taking their name from the expression we have of 'backend' for later in the year, and bannut, the dialect name for walnut. The young walnuts are just about ready for pickling this month, and many a youngster received a couple of strokes of the cane for going to school with stained fingers from peeling them — the master swearing that it was tobacco stain. However, in this recipe the walnuts do not have to be peeled, but will still stain your hands, so wear rubber gloves if you do not fancy having to pumice stone them clean!

Young walnuts still in their shells
1 tablesp cloves
Brine, made of 3 ozs salt to a pint of water, enough to cover the quantity of walnuts picked
2 onions to each pint of vinegar used
1 tablesp peppercorns
1 tablesp of white sugar to each pint of spiced vinegar, if you like a sweet pickled walnut

Prick the shells of the washed walnuts all over with a steel thin needle. Place in a bowl and cover with the brine. Let stand for a total of 10 days, changing the brine every two days. Drain well, then lay on trays in the open air until the walnuts are black. Boil the vinegar with the spices and finely chopped onion, and sugar if used. Pack the walnuts in jars and strain the vinegar over. When cold, cover and seal. These make excellent presents for Christmas when they are really mature.

October

Cooks in Books — Food Links The Festivals

October brings the second Horse Fair of the year at Stow-on-the-Wold, a colourful occasion when dealers have the horses showing their paces in the wide streets. It is one of the biggest markets in the country specialising in horses, and the atmosphere is busy with banter and barter, charged with the dialect and secret language of the centuries-old trade. The Fair fare is traditional to other parts of the Cotswolds, and the only reference to that of the old market town is to be found in a ballad of 1641 recounting the wonders of Dick Whittington and his cat:

At Stow on the Wold
The wind blows cold
And the cooks have nothing to cook

Not a very inspiring proverb. However, the month also sees the Literary Festival at Cheltenham and the Stroud Arts Festival, so it is the Cotswold fare and links with some of the nation's finest writers that provide the food for thought for this month.

The Alice, which Lewis Carroll immortalised in her Wonderland and Through The Looking Glass, was Alice Liddell whose uncle was Rector of Cowley near Cheltenham. Laurie Lee's childhood is equally as captivating and famous, and one can almost smell the warm steam and smoke in his descriptions of the cottage kitchen in the Slad Valley. Mrs Craik sets much of *John Halifax, Gentleman*, at Rose Cottage in the hillside hamlet of Amberley, and Jane Austen's pen dips into Bath. Charles Dickens has adorable old Pickwick dining at Tewkesbury, and even the dour old radical, William Cobbett came this way in his *Rural Rides*. Other travellers have made notes of their journeys and the hostelries, and Shakespeare made famous the pungency of Tewkesbury mustard. J Arthur Gibbs, whose book *A Cotswold Village*, has withstood the test of time and survived the vagaries of fashion, comments on the Cotsaller's diet of bread and bacon, the fine trout and apple dumplings and the cottager's pig; and John Taylor, the Water Poet, spoke of Gloucestershire's Bag Puddings.

Beatrix Potter first visited Harescombe Grange, the home of her cousin, in 1894. It was here that she heard the tale of the *Tailor of Gloucester* and turned it into a world-wide classic. Millions of children, and adults who never outgrow the charm of 'once upon a time', know that Simpkin was sent into the streets of Gloucester with the tailor's last groat and a china pipkin to 'buy a penn'orth of bread, a penn'orth of milk and a penn'orth of sausages...'. Gloucester sausage is nearly as famous as the cherry-coloured silk (which Simpkin was to have bought with the last penny of the groat).

Perhaps the last word belongs to our first poet, Geoffrey Chaucer who married Phillipa, sister of Catherine Swynford — the mistress and later wife of John of Gaunt, whose first wife, Lady Blanche of Lancaster, was Chaucer's patroness. Chaucer lived at Kempsford, under Lady Blanche's patronage in the mid-14th century. He said of the Cook — A Pilgrim to Canterbury:

They had a cook with them who stood alone

For boiling chicken with a marrow-bone
Sharp flavouring — powder and spice for savour
He could distinguish London ale by flavour,
And he could roast and seethe and broil and fry,
Make good thick soup and bake a tasty pie.

Mock Turtle Soup

. . . Beautiful Soup! Who cares for fish,
Game, or any other dish?
Who would not give all else for
Two pennyworth only of beautiful soup . . .

Poor old Mock Turtle — no wonder he sobbed when he sang this song for Alice in Wonderland, but then Mock Turtle soup is not made of mock turtles any more than shepherd's pie is made of shepherds. Two pennyworth would have been a goodly helping of Mock Turtle Soup made to Mrs Beeton's recipe, which she costed — in the days when one could actually put prices in cookery books — as 2s.6d. to serve 10 or 12 persons. This version is the more luxurious of the two she gives.

½ a calf's head
¼ lb butter
½ lb lean ham
2 tablesps minced parsley
a little minced lemon thyme, sweet marjoram and basil
2 onions
a few chopped mushrooms
2 shallots
2 tablesps flour
¼ bottle Madeira or sherry
12 forcemeat balls (sausagemeat)
cayenne, salt and mace to taste
juice of 1 lemon and 1 Seville orange
1 dessertsp pounded sugar (use caster)
3 quarts of good stock

Scald the head with the skin on, remove the brain, tie the head up in a cloth and let it boil for 1 hour. Then take the meat from the bones, cut it into small square pieces and throw them into cold water. Now take the meat, put into a stewpan and cover with stock; let it boil gently for an hour, or rather more if not quite tender and set it on one side. Melt the butter in another stewpan and add the ham, cut small, with the herbs, parsley, shallots, mushrooms and nearly a pint of stock; let these simmer slowly for 2 hours and then dredge in as much flour as will dry up the butter. Fill up with the remainder of the stock, add the wine, let it stew gently for 10 minutes, rub it through a tammy (sieve it) and put it to the calf's head; season with cayenne and, if required, a little salt; add the juice of the orange and lemon and when liked, ¼ teaspoonful of pounded mace and the sugar. Put in the forcemeat balls, simmer 5 minutes and serve very hot.

Note: the bones of the head should be well stewed in the liquor it was first boiled in; and will make a good white stock, flavoured with vegetables.

Lentil And Tomato Soup

Laurie Lee's recollection of lentil stew which fed the large family doesn't sound nearly as good as this soup made with fresh tomatoes and only a small proportion of potato and lentils to thicken it.

(Serves 6)
1 lb ripe tomatoes
l onion
1 medium potato
2 ozs butter
4 ozs lentils
2 teasps celery salt
2 level teasps caster sugar
freshly ground black pepper
1½ pint white or chicken stock

Slice the potato and chop the onion, then fry together in a large pan with the butter for about 5 minutes to soften. Grind the lentils down and add, with the stock to the pan. Stir in to blend, cover and simmer for about 1 hour, stirring occasionally. Peel and chop the tomatoes, add with the seasoning and sugar and simmer together for a further 10 minutes. When cool enough, liquidise to make a completely smooth soup. Re-heat, but do not allow to boil.

Skimmerlad

Skimmerlad is the Cotswold word for a stew which has a dumpling dough cover all over the top. It probably evolved as a kind of edible lid for the great cast iron open pots suspended on a hook and chain over an open fire. The 'dump' top is cut in wedges to serve with the stew, but, if preferred, dumplings can be made instead to add to the stew for the last 20 minutes of the cooking time. Whichever method you choose, this dish could well be the 'big pots of stew' which Laurie Lee says of his childhood memories that 'he called for in the night'.

(Serves 6)
2 lbs shin beef
2 level tablesps seasoned flour
8 ozs onions, sliced
2 ozs beef dripping
½ pint cider
1 pint beef stock
8 ozs carrots, diced
8 ozs turnips, diced
2 sticks celery, diced

for the dump:
2 ozs self-raising flour
2 ozs fresh white breadcrumbs
2 tablesps shredded suet
1 tablesp chopped parsley
1 egg, beaten lightly
seasoning

Cut and trim the meat into l-inch cubes and coat in the seasoned flour. Heat the dripping in a large pan and fry the onions gently until soft and not browned, then add the meat and fry until brown all over. Stir in the cider and stock and season to taste. Bring to the boil, then add the vegetables and reduce the heat, cover with a lid and simmer for about 2 hours. Make the skimmerlad — or dumplings — by mixing all ingredients together with a wooden spoon. Mould between floured hands either as one 'lid' to fit on top of the stewpan, or into 6 equally sized dumplings. Place on top of the stew, removing the lid to cook them. They will cook through the steam, so do not need to be turned over. Simmer for a further 20-30 minutes. Serve immediately.

Collared Beef

Eighteenth century travellers were just as critical of the food and service at the posting houses they visited as we are today of hotels and eating places — although, of course, there were fewer of them who had either the means or the inclination to roam too far from their home comforts. The ubiquitous Hon. John Byng awarded only 10 posting houses on his tour of 530 miles the distinction of 'Good' — the ancient Bull at Fairford being one of them, on his visit in 1787. George Phillips was mine host and Byng spoke highly of his civility and that of his staff and the dinner which followed, which included 'cold boil'd beef rowl'd up as tho' collar'd'. If it was anything like this recipe for collared beef in a red wine jelly, then the praise was duly earned.

(Serves 10-12)
5-6 lb boned and rolled fore-rib of beef
1 pint red wine
1 pkt gelatine
3 bay leaves
¼ teasp mixed spice
¼ teasp dried thyme
¼ teasp dried sage
10 cloves
1 onion, chopped
1 clove garlic, crushed
fresh parsley and radishes to garnish
seasoning

Get the butcher to bone and roll the beef. Wipe with a paper towel and trim off any excess fat on the edges. Shake salt and pepper over the joint, then rub in the spice and dried herbs all over with your hands. Put the spiced beef into a deep bowl and add the cloves, onion and garlic. Pour the wine over and cover with a cloth, weighted with a plate or board. Leave to marinate overnight, turning the meat over a couple of times. Pour the entire contents into a large pan and bring to the boil. Cover with a lid then simmer for 3-3½ hours. Allow to cool in the liquid, then drain the beef and put into a deep dish. Fit a plate on top and weight down with an iron or bags of sugar to press. Chill for at least 8 hours, but keep the cooking liquor. To make the red wine jelly, strain the cooking liquor into a clean pan and bring rapidly to the boil. Keep at boiling point for 3 minutes. Dissolve the gelatine in a little of the wine, then add the remainder and pour into a jug. Taste for seasoning and add more at this point if it needs it. When on the point of setting, slice the beef and arrange on a large serving dish. Spoon the jelly carefully over to cover each slice to form a glaze. When set, garnish with radish roses and sprigs of fresh parsley.

Steak And Kidney Pudding

When Laurie Lee walked out one midsummer morning from his Slad Valley home he describes the meals he had in the early days in London. He says: 'My favourite was the pie — a little basin of meat wrapped in a caul of suety dough which was kept boiling all day in a copper cauldron in a cupboard under the stairs'. Strictly speaking the 'pie' was a pudding if it was boiled. So here is an ages-old recipe for Cotswold's favourite author for his favourite 'pie'.

(Serves 4)
8 ozs self-raising flour
4 ozs shredded beef suet
large pinch salt about
¼ pint cold water
12 ozs chuck steak
4 ozs ox kidney
1 medium onion
1 oz plain flour
4 tablesps stock
4 ozs mushrooms, sliced

Make a suet crust pastry by mixing the self-raising flour and salt, together with the suet in a basin. Add enough water to make a firm but pliable dough, mixing with a knife rather than a spoon. Knead lightly on a floured board and cut off a quarter to make the lid. Grease a 1½ pint sized pudding basin and roll out the larger piece of pastry to fit. Line carefully and trim the top close to the rim. Press the pastry lightly against the sides of the basin to hold it in place while you fill it. Cut the meat into small dice and slice the kidney finely. Peel and finely chop the onion and mix in a basin with the meat and scatter with the plain flour, toss to coat the meat evenly, then add the mushrooms.

Tip into the pastry-lined basin and add enough stock to meanly cover. Roll the rest of the suet pastry out lightly and place on top, pinching the edges together to seal. Trim the edges. Cover with greased paper or foil, and tie on a clean white pudding cloth with fine string round the rim of the basin. Bring the corners of the cloth to the top and knot opposite ends to the middle — like an old-time traveller's knotted handkerchief on his walking stick. Steam for 4½ hours, or boil in a large pan for 3½ hours, making sure that the water is boiling when you put the pudding in and you keep it topped up with boiling water during the cooking time. Serve hot straight from the basin, with creamed potatoes and boiled carrots.

Tewkesbury Ham

'At the Hop Pole at Tewkesbury they stopped to dine', so wrote Charles Dickens in *The Pickwick Papers*, if they had been served home-cured ham, pickled the Tewkesbury way, then indeed they may have had cause to 'sing duets in the dickey' afterwards.

This pickling process is taken from a very old method:

Rub thoroughly for ten consecutive days, daily, with salt, if the ham be a twenty-pounder. Place in a milk pan or other large receptacle, and mix thoroughly one and a half ounces saltpetre, one ounce bay salt, one ounce black pepper, one and a half ounces black treacle. When the above ingredients are thoroughly blended, baste your ham with them twice a day for three weeks. Now remove from the pickle, and hang a full day to drain. Smoke in peat. Allow two months to mature. Soak in cold water for twelve hours. Thus prepared, this ham will, with reasonable precautions, keep indefinitely. Now make a paste of flour and water, coat the ham with the paste, and bake, allowing twenty minutes to the pound.

The following follows the traditional method, but adapted for today's cook. It is still worth curing your own ham, which the butcher will get fresh for you, given sufficient notice. This pickle renders a sweet taste to the ham which is absolutely delicious.

14 lbs fresh ham, specify that you want to cure it yourself
3½ lbs table salt (free-running)

for the brine:
1 lb sea salt (crystals)
1½ ozs allspice
3 ozs black peppercorns, ground
12 ozs golden syrup
8 ozs plain Cotswold honey
8 pints cold water

for the dough crust and final baking:
3 lbs plain flour
4 ozs demerara sugar
about 10 cloves

Wipe the ham with a damp cloth then lay it on a large flat dish. Rub half the table salt into it all over, then cover completely with the rest of the table salt. Leave in a cold place for 24 hours, as the salt turns to liquid, rub this back into the ham a couple of times. Prepare the pickling brine by putting all the ingredients together in a large pan. Bring to the boil, then remove from the heat, cover the pan and leave to get quite cold. Drain the ham from its salt and wipe dry with a cloth. Put into an earthenware crock and pour the pickling brine over. Cover and let stand for 12 hours. Remove the ham and once more cover with a thin layer of the table salt. Leave another 12 hours. Boil the brine up again and when quite cold put the ham back into it and leave this time for 10 days, covered in a cold place, turning the ham in the brine at least once a day to ensure that it is evenly soaked. Rinse the brine off after the long steeping, then let it soak in cold water for a couple of hours to remove the excess saltiness.

To bake the ham:

Make a stiff dough with the 3 lb of plain flour and water. Roll out to about ¼-inch thickness large enough to encase the whole ham. Thoroughly dry the ham by wiping with a dry cloth and lay on the paste. Draw up and seal all edges with water. Bake on a large baking tray in a pre-heated oven at 180°C (Gas Mark 4) for 3 hours. Remove from the oven and break off the crust. Remove the skin from the ham and rub in the brown sugar, stick in the cloves, then increasing the heat by 2 marks, bake for a further 10 minutes to set and crisp the sugary crust. Leave to get quite cold before serving.

Family Rice Pudding

This is rich, but light, and worthy of being one of our national dishes.

(Serves 4-6)
1 pint milk
2 ozs short grain rice
3 ozs caster sugar
2 eggs, separated
about ½ oz butter
about ⅓ nutmeg, grated

Wash the rice in a sieve and boil in just enough water to cover, for about 5 minutes. Drain off any excess water and tip the rice into a buttered 2-pint sized ovenproof dish. Stir in the milk with 2 tablespoons of the sugar. Flake the butter on top, then grate the nutmeg over. Bake in a pre-heated oven at 170°C (Gas Mark 3) for about 1 hour. Remove from the oven and let cool for about 5 minutes, then beat in the egg yolks lightly. Cook for a further 30 minutes. Whisk the egg whites until stiff and fold in the rest of the sugar. Take the pudding out of the oven, and again cool for 5 minutes before folding the whipped egg white mixture through the pudding, make sure it is well blended but folded in lightly. Sprinkle with a little more nutmeg and cook for a further 15 minutes until the pudding is set. Serve with warmed jam as a sauce, or accompaniment to baked apples.

Tantadlin

This is the Cotswold word, used very infrequently now, more's the pity, for Apple Dumpling. J Arthur Gibbs, in his classic portrayal of *A Cotswold Village* as it was at the end of last century, relates the advice given by the famous Dr Johnson to his friends, always to have a good orchard attached to their houses. 'For,' said he, 'I once knew a clergyman of small income who brought up a family very reputably, which he chiefly fed on apple dumplings'. Many a Cotswold family has been brought up very reputably on Tantadlin.

(Serves 4)
8 ozs self-raising flour
4 ozs shredded suet
pinch of salt
about ¼ pint cold water
4 cooking apples
4 cloves
4 dessertsps sugar
about ½ oz butter

Make a suet crust by mixing the flour, salt and suet together with enough cold water to form a smooth and pliable dough. Cut into four pieces. Roll out each piece lightly on a floured board. Peel and core the apples. Stand an apple on the centre of each piece of pastry and fill the centre with sugar, pressing down with the end of a wooden spoon. Cut a slither of butter to put on top and insert a clove. Brush the edges of the pastry with water and gather round the apple, bring to the top and pinch together to completely seal. Tie each dumpling in a well-floured pudding cloth and lower into a pan of boiling water. Keep boiling, replenishing the water with more boiling water as it evaporates, for 45-50 minutes. Serve hot with custard.

Baked Apple Dumplings With Plum Sauce

This is a rather more superior pudding, which no doubt will be called a dessert, or sweet, when served to guests.

(Serves 4)
4 large dessert apples
1 lb puff pastry
4 ozs white marzipan
1 egg, lightly beaten
1 lb ripe red plums, stoned
2 ozs granulated sugar
1 tablesp lemon juice
mint leaves to garnish
couple of drops of almond essence

Cut the pastry into quarters and roll out each piece on a floured board just large enough to encase the apples. Peel and core the apples and stand in the centre of the pastry squares. Cut the marzipan into four pieces and roll each into a plug to fill the centre of the apples. Brush the edges of the pastry with the lightly beaten egg and draw up to the top and pinch to seal. Place, seal side down, on a greased baking sheet. Roll out the trimming from the pastry and cut three small leaf shapes for each dumpling, brush with egg to seal, then completely glaze each dumpling with the remaining egg. Chill for 15 minutes while pre-heating the oven to 190°C (Gas Mark 5). Bake for about 40 minutes until the pastry is puffed up and golden brown and the apples are tender when pierced with a skewer. Make the sauce by stewing the plums with the sugar in a mere thread of water to prevent sticking until they are very soft. Puree or liquidise until smooth, then add lemon juice to taste, together with a couple of spots of almond essence. Spoon the sauce on individual serving plates and place the baked apple dumpling on top. Can be served hot or cool — but best not left to get really cold.

Gloucester Sausage

The Gloucester Sausage is a plumper, longer version of its '8 to a pound' cousins. Many family butchers have devised their own recipes over the years to appease their customers' taste, but the traditional Gloucester Sausage is easy enough to make at home if you cannot find it in speciality butchers. Your family butcher may be able to get the skins for you — if not, they lose nothing of their taste if they are skinless — rolled into shape, floured and fried as normal. In any case, once you have tasted 'the real thing', it will be hard to revert to the pale, watery unbeknown that lurk in sausage skins in the supermarket.

(Makes about 18 good-sized sausages)
2 lbs very lean pork, finely minced
8 ozs fresh white breadcrumbs
12 ozs shredded suet - try to get beef suet and mince yourself
¼ teasp grated nutmeg
1 teasp finely chopped sage
½ teasp finely chopped thyme
½ teasp finely chopped marjoram
1½ teasps salt
sausage skins (or flour to shape the mixture)
about ½ teasp freshly ground black pepper

Note: if fresh herbs are not available use the same quantities (but meanly measured) of dried herbs

Put all the ingredients together in a big bowl and mix well to distribute the herbs and seasoning evenly. If using skins, fill a forcing bag with the mixture and attach a long, wide nozzle. Knot the end of the skin about 3 feet in length and push the nozzle through the skin as close to the knot as possible. Force the sausagemeat through, withdrawing as the skin fills — do not overfill otherwise the skins will burst when cooking. When the length is filled, knot the end. Twist the filled skin at intervals to the length of sausage required. Tie a piece of string into a loop about half way along the length of sausages and hang up on a hook in a cool place for an hour or two to allow the sausagemeat to settle in the skins before cutting at the twists and frying as normal.

Cotswold Cream Cheese

The Rural Rides of William Cobbett brought him to the Cotswolds in 1826; he had little good to say of the countryside which he described as 'ugly country' — it seems as if the stone brash put him off as he enthused about the lush pastureland of the Vale. Most of his observations were soured by his political purpose, but every now and again he found some aspect to delight his dour old senses as when he visited the last Gloucestershire parish on his route and at Mr Arkell's dairy farm at Kempsford saw 'a fine dairy and a cheese loft with, perhaps, more than two thousand cheeses in it; at least there were many hundreds'.

The dairy was very much a part of the Cotswold scene over a hundred years ago and my next recipe comes from one of the most famous farming families in Cotswold's history. It was the Garne family at Aldsworth that saved the ancient breed of Cotswold sheep from extinction — and even the crusty old Cobbett was impressed by their size and stature.

Mrs A E Garne's Cream Cheese (about 1870)

5 pints of new milk and 1 pint of cream made rather warmer than milk fresh from the cow; put about 3 dessertspoonfuls of rennet (or according to the strength of the rennet) to turn it and let it stand for about 20 minutes, or half an hour. Put a cloth into a sieve and put the curd into it with a skimmer, let it stand for a few minutes then put a cloth into a hoop and place the curd into it. Fold the cloth over the top and place on it a 3-4 lb weight, just to press it. Let it remain for an hour or two then change into a clean cloth and hoop and let it stay until the next morning. It must then have the cloth taken off and be sprinkled with a little salt on both sides. Put a binder round it and leaves on both sides. It must be turned and have fresh leaves and a binder every morning. The cheese will be ready in about 10 days. If put between pewter plates it will be hastened in getting fit. Strawberry young plant or raspberry leaves are the best to use. If approved, more cream and less milk may be used.

Home Sweet Treacle Biscuits

Laurie Lee left his Slad Valley home at the age of 19 to seek his fortune in the wide world beyond his native Cotswold hills. He describes, as only Laurie Lee can, how 'As I walked Out One Midsummer Morning' his only belongings he took were 'a small rolled-up tent, a violin in a blanket, a change of clothes and a tin of treacle biscuits', which, when he ate them later, sitting on an old stone wall 'I could hear mother banging the kettle on the hob and my brothers rattling their tea-cups. The treacle biscuits tasted sweetly of the honeyed squalor of home...'

Treacle biscuits nearly defeated me — but I eventually found a recipe among the handwritten notes in a little book belonging to Miriam Jane Pedley of Bibury, dated 1868. Typical of the many recipe notebooks devised for personal use, there are many details assumed, or known by heart so never needing to be recorded, such as, in this case, the baking temperature or for how long. However, with some trial and error, I have merely altered the original 'bake in a cold oven' to what will actually bake the biscuits. The rest of the recipe is as written over a hundred years ago in a Cotswold kitchen.

Take:

2 lbs flour
¾ lb butter
1 lb moist sugar (use soft brown)
1½ ozs ginger
1 lb treacle (use black treacle, not golden syrup)
2 ozs lemon peel

Mix the whole together, roll it thin and bake in a pre-heated oven at 190°C (Gas Mark 5) for 7-10 minutes. Remove carefully with a fish slice to cool and harden on a wire tray.

Muffins

According to The Baker's Tale, 'They roused him with muffins ...' when *Hunting the Snark*. Well! If the sneaky old Snark could not be roused with muffins, then he must have been a Boojum! Anyway, there are few words which conjure up a cosy tea by the fireside as 'Muffins'. The Muffin Man was a popular figure as he visited the towns and villages with a wooden tray on his head and ringing his bell — another character lost as the Second World War wrought changes in our way of living forever. But, for the willing cook there is a chance to recreate the smell of warm, fresh muffins in your own kitchen again. The traditional way to cook them is on a heavy iron griddle, but a heavy-based frying pan will do — or they can be baked in the oven.

(Makes 10 muffins)

10 ozs strong white flour
1 teasp salt
½ oz fresh yeast
1 tablesp olive or sunflower oil
8-10 fl ozs warm water

Sieve the flour and salt together and put to warm until the flour feels warm to the touch. Dissolve the sugar in about 7 fl ozs of the warm water and spoon out 2 tablespoons to mix with the yeast. Stir in the rest of the sugar and water mixture. Tip the warmed flour into a warmed mixing bowl and make a well in the centre. Pour in the yeast mixture and the oil and blend vigorously, adding a little more warm water if necessary to make a soft dough which will hold its shape. Knead to an elastic texture, then mould into a rough ball shape and put to rise, covered with greased polythene, for 1 hour. Cut into 10 equally sized pieces. Mould each into a ball and rest on a thickly floured board for a second rising. Dredge flour quite thickly on the tops and again cover with polythene, leave in a warm place for another 30 minutes.

The mufins can then be cooked either on a lightly oiled griddle, or pan, for about 6 minutes over a medium heat, turn over and cook for a similar time on the other side. If you can get the round metal rings in which to put the muffins before they are cooked, the better will be the shape. To oven bake muffins, place on greased heavy oven plates, previously heated, and cook in a pre-heated oven at 220°C (Gas Mark 7) for about 10 minutes, turn them over and cook the other side for a further 10 minutes.

Muffins should never be cut with a knife, just split open, butter lavishly and spread with creamy Cotswold honey.

Bath Buns

The south-westerly tip of the Cotswold escarpment provides the wooded bowl in which the City of Bath nestles, at once Roman and Regency, and here one thinks of Jane Austen, taking tea with sedate young ladies and drinking in the atmosphere as they toyed with their Bath Buns and Sally Lunns. Bath City folk rightly claim that Bath Buns are only those made in the City itself, and others by that name are 'London Bath Buns' — (irrespective of where they are made). So, a Bath Bun, by any other name, can be made quite easily at home.

(Makes 16)

For the dough:
10 ozs strong white flour
3 ozs softened (not oily) butter
1 oz granulated sugar
4 ozs sultanas
1 oz candied lemon peel, chopped
finely grated rind of 1 lemon
6 ozs lump sugar, crushed roughly with a rolling pin, or coffee crystals
1 egg, beaten

For the ferment:
2 ozs strong white flour
1 egg, lightly beaten
2 teasps white sugar
¾ oz fresh yeast
about ¼ pint warm water

Prepare the ferment first by stirring the egg with the warm water to make up 7 ½ fl ozs of liquid, warm to the touch. Stir in the sugar and when it is dissolved, spoon out 3 tablespoons of the liquid to mix the yeast to a smooth paste in a large bowl. Add the rest of the liquid, then whisk in the flour until it is batter like in consistency. Cover with polythene and leave in a warm place to rise for 30 minutes. Make the dough by sieving the flour into a large bowl; making a well in the centre, spoon in the granulated sugar, then pour the ferment on top of the sugar, stirring until it is dissolved. Gradually draw in the flour from the edges and work until a smooth dough is formed. Now knead the butter into the dough, a little at a time. Mould into a round ball shape, put in a warm, greased bowl, covering with greased polythene, to rise in a warm place for about 1 hour. The dough should be about three times its original size. Turn out onto a lightly floured board and spoon the candied peel, lemon rind and 4 ozs of the crushed sugar on top. Knead well in so that they are well incorporated. The dough should be quite smooth. Cover again with polythene and leave for 7 minutes. Pull into 16 pieces — do not cut with a knife — space well apart on a warmed and well buttered baking sheet. Cover with the polythene and put to rise for another 20 minutes. Brush the tops with the lightly beaten egg and scatter the rest of the crushed sugar over. Put in a warm place for the final proving — uncovered this time, for another 20 minutes. Bake in a pre-heated oven at 230°C (Gas Mark 8) for about 10 minutes when the buns should be a rich golden colour. Serve, split open with the fingers, if liked, and buttered, although they are delicious plain.

Sally Lunn

A Sally Lunn is really a sweet bread, often called a bun or a cake. Named after Sally Lunn who lived in Bath and baked her golden round breads in Lilliput Alley in the 1780s, they became very popular with the rich and gouty gentry who came to Bath to take the waters. Her little shop, on the site of a Roman building some 2,000 years old, still sells the famous Sally Lunn. But if you can't get there for these quite delicious little loaves, then you can make them yourself in the comfort of your own kitchen. They should be eaten freshly cooked, as soon as they are cool enough to split open — with a knife — and spread liberally with butter. Powdered cinnamon and brown sugar make a treat as a topping.

(Makes 3 in 5-inch round cake tins)

For the dough:
10 ozs strong white flour
1½ ozs white sugar
1 egg, lightly beaten
the grated rind of 1 lemon
2 ozs softened butter

For the ferment:
2 ozs strong white flour
¾ oz fresh yeast
2 level teasps white sugar
about ¼ pt warm water

Make the ferment by blending the flour, yeast and sugar together with the water added gradually to make a thin, smooth paste. Set to rise in a warm place, covered with greased polythene, for 20 minutes. Prepare the dough by sieving the flour into a large bowl, making a well in the centre. Put the sugar, most of the beaten egg (save a little for the glaze), and the lemon rind in the well, pour on the ferment and stir until well blended. Draw in the flour and mix to a smooth dough. Knead, then knead in the softened butter. Make into a large ball shape and put to rise in a lightly buttered bowl, under greased polythene, for 30 minutes. Divide into 3 pieces, shape each into a round ball and place in warmed and lightly buttered tins. Cover and leave again to rise for 20 minutes. Brush the tops with the egg, mixed with a little milk if necessary, cover and leave for a further 20 minutes while pre-heating the oven to 230°C (Gas Mark 8). Bake for 15 minutes.

Schoolroom Sweets

Village schools provided the only large communal building for any social events as may be held, outside the church before village halls came into being. In *John Halifax, Gentleman*, Mr Guy 'had gone off to the school tea-drinking ...' These sweets would have featured at many a school treat in the Cotswolds in the days when everything had to be home-made.

1 medium sized cold boiled potato
1 lb icing sugar
12 glace cherries, chopped
about 4 ozs walnuts, chopped
a few drops of almond or lemon essence

Mash down the cold potato then knead in all the other ingredients until a very stiff paste is formed. Roll out onto a board, dusted with icing sugar and leave to harden for about 10 hours. The paste can then be cut into small squares or stamped out in small shapes with a cutter. Dust over with a little more sieved icing sugar.

Tea-drinking was a great social occasion when it was introduced in the 18th century, and bowls preceded cups as the vessel from which to drink the then very expensive brew. George III, on his visit to Sudeley Castle, refreshed himself with a 'dish of tea', but then fell down a staircase so didn't stop. It is estimated that as a nation of tea-drinkers we now brew up some 440 million pounds of tea in a year.

Taking milk in tea was first observed by a Dutchman in China in 1655, but the idea did not take on here for more than a century. In fact, according to a receipt from *The Closet of Sir Kenhelm Digby, Kt., Opened,* dated 1671, eggs were mixed with tea. I include it here as the timing beats all those little running sands timers, and certainly all the pingers and dingers that measure time for the cook today.

Tea With Eggs (1671)

To near a pint of tea take two yolks of new-laid eggs and beat them very fine with as much fine sugar as is sufficient for this quantity of liquor. When they are very well mixed pour your tea on the eggs and sugar and stir them together. In these parts we let the hot water remain too long soaking upon the tea. The water is to remain on the tea no longer than whiles you can say the Miserere Psalm very slowly.

Home-brewed wines have been a much longer heritage and cottage walls have dripped with the heady steam of Cotswold hedgerow and garden for centuries. Nothing was ever wasted, and Laurie Lee in his classic tale of his Cotswold valley childhood conjures up the picture in Cider With Rosie: '*what seasons fermented in Granny Wallon's kitchen, what summers were brought to the boil ... And not only flower-heads went into these brews; the old lady used parsnips, too, potatoes, sloes . . .*'

Potato Wine

(Yields about 8 pints)
4 lbs old potatoes
12 pints cold water
3 lbs best demerara sugar
1 lemon
1 orange
1-inch piece of root ginger
1 oz wine (or baker's) yeast

Wash the potatoes well but do not peel them, cut into very small cubes and put in a large pan with the water. Bring to the boil and cook until the potatoes are soft but not broken. Strain the liquid into a large crock and add the sugar, slice the fruit thinly into it, add the ginger and stir until the sugar has dissolved completely. Return to the pan and simmer for 30 minutes. Leave to cool to lukewarm then strain into a fermentation jar, not more than three-quarters full. Break up the yeast and crumble into the jar. Fit with an airlock and let stand in a cool place until the fermentation has ceased, rack and bottle. Let mature for at least 6 months before opening.

Sloe Wine, Bessie Pedley, Bibury (1868)

To one quart of water put one quart of sloes. Boil slowly and when they begin to crack, take them out with a skimmer and let them drain (do not squeeze them). To every gallon of liquor, add 3½ lbs of loaf sugar, and strain through a flannel bag. Put into the cask when cold. In 3 months rack off.

Sloe Gin

Compared with the long process of making wine, the age-old method of adding fruit to cheap gin is quick and easy. Of course, one starts with the alcohol, whereas with wine-making it is a case of inducing fermentation. Raspberry Gin can be made earlier in the year in the same way. Sloes, bullaces and wild plum are hard, sharp fruits of the hedgerow that make the best type of liquor; ruby-red and sweet, it is a potent reminder of sun-drenched country lanes when opened in the glow of a winter's fireside.

1 pint cheap gin
about 1 lb granulated sugar
2-3 lbs sloes

Pick the sloes after the first frost has softened them. Wash thoroughly and prick all over with a sterilized steel needle. Almost half fill screw-top bottles with the fruit. Add enough sugar to just cover, then fill the bottle with the gin. Leave in a dry, dark place for six weeks, shaking the bottle, and turning upside down carefully once or twice a week to dissolve the sugar. At the end of this time the juices should have run freely and the gin turned a warm ruby-red colour. Strain into a jug, then pour into smaller bottles to seal ready for Christmas — a small bottle of sloe gin makes a very special gift for close friends. Do not discard the fruit — it will be liquor-soaked by now and could be frozen for use later. Use, simmered until very soft, then sieved to make a purée base for home-made ice cream or desserts, or sweet sauce for meats.

Home Made Tewkesbury Hot Mustard

The mustard seeds were, it is reputed, once ground down with cannon balls because they were so hard.

4 tablesps mustard seed
12 cloves
12 allspice berries
10 black peppercorns
4 dried chillis
10 white peppercorns
1 teasp coriander
1 teasp ground ginger
1 teasp cayenne pepper
1 teasp turmeric
1 teasp paprika pepper
1 teasp coarse salt
15-16 tablesps white wine vinegar

Today's cooks do not need to go looking for stray cannon balls to grind down the mustard seeds — an electric grinder does the job in no time, or a pestle and mortar can be used without too much effort. Grind the mustard seeds down a tablespoon at a time because it is better to have a mixture of different textures. Grind each tablespoon of seeds to a degree coarser than the previous, so that the seed varies from quite coarse, coarse, moderate and powdery. Tip into a basin. Now grind the seeds from the chillis (the pods can be kept for flavouring other dishes) and rough grind the peppercorns, cloves, coriander seeds and the allspice berries — don't reduce them to powder, leave a good bit of texture to each. Add the rest of the dry ingredients and stir to thoroughly mix the spices together. Now mix in the vinegar, a spoonful at a time and stir well each time. The mustard should be wet but not sloppy, with a tiny bit of loose vinegar floating on the top when you press the mixture down lightly with the back of the spoon.

When completely blended, pack into small jars right to the top, cover tightly to exclude the air, and seal down. Store for 4-5 weeks in a cool, dark and dry place, then it is ready for use.

Cotswold Mustard Pickle

This is very much like piccalilli and has the advantage of making use of a good variety of vegetables from the garden. Use small onions or shallots and, if using cauliflower, make sure that you break it into tiny florets. Each piece of the pickle should be bite size and should never need cutting on the plate.

2 lbs mixed vegetables, prepared weight: choose from cauliflower, small onions or shallots, gherkins, green beans, small cucumber, courgettes, small green tomatoes on the point of 'turning', vegetable marrow, peppers, celery
1 pint vinegar
4 level tablesps granulated sugar
1 level teasp dry mustard
½ level tablesp turmeric
½ level tablesp ground ginger
1 level tablesp cornflour
1 oz pickling spice
about 4 ozs salt

Prepare the vegetables and cut into small chunks, spread out on a large dish and scatter about 1 oz of salt over. Leave to start softening the vegetables, for 4 hours, then rinse and put into a deep bowl. Make a brine to just cover the vegetables, using 2 ozs salt to each pint of water. Cover and let stand overnight. Drain and pack into dry jars. Make the mustard sauce by blending the cornflour with a little of the vinegar to make a smooth paste, then adding the rest, stirring to prevent lumps. Put into a pan with the rest of the spices and the sugar. Bring just to boiling point, then reduce heat instantly and keep at simmering point until the sauce thickens, about 15 minutes. Leave to cool slightly, then pour the hot mixture over the vegetables in the jars, covering to the rim. Cover and seal immediately. Make sure that the seal is airtight. Leave in a cool, dry and dark store for 3 weeks to allow the flavours to mingle and the vegetables to soften a little more. Eat within about 1 month once opened.

Mustard and Herb Dressing

½ teasp mustard powder
½ teasp salt
½ teasp white pepper
1 level teasp caster sugar
6 tablesps sunflower oil
rind and juice of ½ large lemon
small bunch of fresh herbs (parsley, chives, thyme), finely chopped

Whisk the mustard powder, seasoning, sugar, oil and lemon juice together in a bowl until cloudy and well blended. Add the lemon rind and herbs, stir well. Use for tossing green salad just before serving, or as a dressing for fish dishes.

Blackberry and Apple Chutney

2 lbs blackberries
2 lbs cooking apples
12 ozs onion
1 lb brown sugar
1 pint white vinegar
3 teasps salt
2 teasps ground ginger
1 teasp ground mace
½ oz dry mustard

Prepare the fruit and onion and rough chop into a pan with the rest of the ingredients. Cook at a simmering pace for about an hour — (if you don't like the pips of blackberries they can be sieved at this stage). Now add the sugar, stir until dissolved then bring to the boil and cook until quite thick and all loose vinegar has been absorbed. Pot in warm jars and seal while hot.

November

Bangers and Clangers and Holywake Bakes — Dumps and Duffs, Dunch and Feggy

Glo'shire has such vunny places
As anyone yere well knows
Wi' its Uley moggies and coaley dumps
Cam wi'its ewes and crows
And they do say Dursley baboons
Do yut thur pap
Wi'out any spoons

Derisive ditties about neighbouring villages were often more good humoured than spiteful in the days when rivalry was rife on grounds of superiority, travel between places being a fairly major undertaking. This is what gave identity to each area of the region and colour and cadence to the dialect. This is borne out in these couple of lines from an old ballad:

'Ov their furrin tongues let travellers brag
Wi' their vifteen names vor a puddin-bag

The Victorians claim to have invented the bolster pudding, but John Taylor, the Gloucester born 'Water Poet' wrote in awe of Nicholas Wood, history's famous glutton, listing among the gourmand's diet "the bag-puddings of Gloucestershire". This dates them to the early 17th century. John Taylor left his native Gloucestershire in his calling as waterman, but returned to study at Oxford and later served on the Thames when his boat was laden with, according to his own words, "a hotch potch or gallimaufrey of Sonnets, Satires and Epigrams. With an ink-horn disputation betwixt a Lawyer and a Poet; and a quarterne of new catched Epigrams caught the last fishing-tide".

The English pudding was obviously something to be remarked upon, not just in nostalgic moments when serving "the Queen, Eliza", as Taylor did, but also by travellers "with their furrin tongue', for Masson, a mid-17th century French writer, recorded:

The English are gluttons at noon and abstinent at night ... Blessed be he that invented pudding, for it is a Manna that hits the palates of all sorts of people. Ah! what an excellent thing is an English pudding! To come in pudding time is as much as to say to come in the most lucky moment in the world.

Puddings come in many guises in Cotswold cookery: there is Hodge Podge, which is a black pudding — a savoury dish; then there are clangers, which are boiled puddings in a bag, also belonging to the savoury class; dumps are boiled puddings' as called 'sweets or desserts', dunch dumps are plain boiled puddings, feggy dumps are richly fruited Christmas puddings, while a duff is like a dump only baked! November is, of course, the month of the bangers — Bonfire Night. The Cotswolds have a special link with old Guy Fawkes for one of the plotters, Robert Gatesby, lived at Chastleton House at one time.

Martinmas, the 11th November, was an important date in the country calendar — long before its now sad remembrance of two world wars. It was a rent day and a day on which the dues were paid, so often the cottager was on the receiving end of long-due debts, affording him a little extra for a feast to 'celebrate the patron saint of beggars, drunkards and outcasts — if he knew at all whom he was celebrating.

It was also the date for pig-killing — a time when the family pig met its end to feed those who had been feeding it for so long. Often the pig was mortgaged to the baker when times were hard, and it was an old saying that someone had killed half a pig! Because the meat had to be cured to keep it for the long winter months and the offal had to be dealt with while still fresh, it was a full family affair, with neighbours often turning a hand to help — exchanging dishes of offal or fresh pig meat, as it was called, for a promise of like return when their great day came round. The favoured time was when there was an 'R' in the month, 'twixt the waxing and the waning of the moon.

Old Cobbett, who gleaned every vestige of country life and living on his *Rural Rides*, said that a man who could not live on solid fat bacon either needed the 'sweet sauce of labour or was fit only for the hospital'. Perhaps fat bacon is not to today's taste, but there are plenty who would, I am sure, welcome a return to the purity and wholesome taste of home-bred bacon, home-cured and home-cooked. So, this month's recipes include those old-time methods. To give some comparison of the cost to the cottager of meat and poultry to buy, here are the prices taken from an old manuscript 600 years ago — in relation to the pittance earned for long hours of hard labour, these were completely beyond his pocket, so the family pig was the more valuable. Even into Edwardian times it was a real hardship if the pig died before it could be killed.

Best roast pig	**8d**
Best roast Capon	**6d**
Pullet, fresh	**2d**
Dunghill mallard	**2d**
3 roast pigeons	**2½d**
Pheasant	**13d**
3 roast thrushes	**2d**
Best roast goose	**7d**
Hen	**4d**
River mallard	**3d**
10 roast finches	**1d**
5 roast larks	**1½d**
Curlew	**6½d**
Rabbit	**4d**
10 eggs	**2d**

(funny! why didn't they lay them in dozens?)

In 1900, when farmworkers wages averaged about 12 shillings a week to raise a whole family, the prices were:

Leg of mutton (to serve 8)	**5s.6d**
Aitchbone of beef per lb	**7d**
Leg of lamb per lb	**1s**
Loin of pork per lb	**10d**
Ham per lb	**10d**
Veal per lb	**1s. ld**
Best salmon per lb	**1s.4d**
8 larks	**2s.6d**
1 rabbit (in skin)	**2s**
1 pheasant	**3s**
3 partridges	**5s**
1 goose	**4s**
1 pigeon	**10d**
2 trout	**2s.6d**

Crowdy

This is the Cotswold word for soup made from pig's head. If you make the stock from it first, then add the pieces of meat which fall off the bones, this gives you a good quantity of stock for the base of other soups.

To make good stock

Clean the bones or carcase and bake them in the oven for about 40 minutes to brown and let any surplus fat run. Take the bones out of the fat and drain on kitchen paper for a short while. Put the bones in a large saucepan with 3 carrots and 3 onions, sliced, a bunch of fresh herbs, a bay leaf and about 6 peppercorns. Fill the pan with water, bring just to the boil, then reduce the heat and keep simmering until the vegetables are cooked. Cool then strain into a bowl or jug. Allow to get quite cold, but do not skim off the fat which will have risen as when this solidifies it seals out the air and keeps the stock beneath it sweet, as we say. Stock will keep for about 3 days in the refrigerator, but it is sensible to freeze any excess to use later. When you are going to use the stock, then scrape the top layer of fat off. By roasting the bones first it gives a better flavour and colour to brown soups or stews, but if a clear soup is required, then omit that process. A lighter stock can be made by just using water in which vegetables have been cooked - the flavour and goodness are still there and it's a pity to throw it away, and it is far less salty and natural than using a commercially produced stock cube.

Crowdy can be made to the quantity you require, so only the basic ingredients are given.

Good stock from the liquid in which the pig's head has simmered
Swedes or turnips
Onions
Carrot
Potatoes
Meat pieces from the bone
a little more herbs of choice
about 2 tablesps pearl barley
2 level tablesps plain flour

Put the prepared vegetables, which should be diced quite small, in the stock and bring just to the boil, reduce the heat then simmer for about 40 minutes. Add the pearl barley and the meat pieces. Continue simmering for a further 20 minutes. Slake the flour with a little water to make a thin paste and stir into the soup. Continue stirring until well blended and thickened. Serve as soon as the pearl barley is tender.

Preparation of pig:

Pre-slaughter care of the animal before taking to the abattoir is essential and humane. It should be given plenty of water to drink, but no food for 24 hours. The pig should be well rested and all excitement avoided, so loading up should be done with plenty of time to spare.

If the pig is not butchered, then these old-time hints on preparation of the carcase are essential.

1. Singe or scald and remove bristles. The base of an old metal candlestick, or holes punched in an old tin will, prove helpful.

2. When singeing, avoid excessive heat otherwise the skin will blister.

3. The offal should be removed within half an hour of slaughtering.

4. The carcase should then be propped open to cool completely before jointing. The village pig-killers used to make a kind of wooden tripod on which to suspend the carcase.

General notes on curing:

Salt is essential in the cure and should be common salt — preferably in the block (it used to be called dairy salt). If the salt is too fine or too coarse it does not penetrate the flesh evenly. It should be perfectly dry.

Saltpetre is not an essential preservative, but was often used to give the bacon a pink colour, although used in excess it would toughen lean meat fibres. It is advisable to mix the curing ingredients together before applying, as this ensures a more even penetration of the cure. Sugar or treacle or molasses give the ham flavour, but the sweetness may attract pests. When removing the ham from dry salt wash off the surplus salt thoroughly, or if too big to handle, it can be wiped over with a cloth wrung out in hot water. Salt should not be left on the meat as it turns to liquid and retards the drying process.

Drying:
Hang the hams to dry in a temperature of around 65°F — a normal room temperature, avoiding direct contact with rays of light. Many old houses, even small cottages, had bacon hooks in the cool stone built larders and many installed bacon racks in the one living room close by the fire to keep it smoke cured. A favourite saying amongst the old folk was, on looking up at drying hams, 'they be the best pictures a man can have a-hanging on 'is wall'.

Storage:
Dust black pepper over the joints, particularly around the bones. Wrap in muslin and seal the joins, or hang in calico bags. Choose a slightly dark place with a good circulation of air.

To prepare bacon for cooking:
Cut off the number of rashers required and pour boiling water over them. Leave for 5 minutes then drain, dry and fry in their own fat. When a joint is wanted for boiling, soak it first in warm water, and change the water quite often over 8 hours, as the salt will be extracted into the water.

Recipe for curing ham is given on page previous page.

Campden Backbone Pie

Chipping Campden's speciality in Cotswold cookery was its famous backbone pie — made of the meaty bones left over from the cutting up of the pig. The fad that there was usually more bone than meat never detracted from the flavour and occasion in the days when a little meant so much.

(Serves 6)
about 1½ lbs of pork pieces on the bone
1 large onion, sliced
½ teasp finely chopped thyme
2 apples, chopped
1 egg, beaten
about 1 oz good dripping
6 ozs self-raising flour
¼ pint stock
4 ozs good lard

Make a shortcrust pastry with the flour and lard and pinch of salt, with enough water to make a pliable, not sticky, dough. Let it rest for 30 minutes while browning the pork pieces, together with the onion in a little dripping. Put with the stock, apples and thyme in a 1½ pint sized pie dish. Cover with the pastry, brush over with the beaten egg, and cut a couple of slits in the lid to allow the steam to escape. Decorate with pastry 'leaves'. Bake in a pre-heated oven at 205°C (Gas Mark 6) for 30 minutes, reduce to 160°C (Gas Mark 3), covering the top if browning too quickly, and cook for a further 45 minutes until the meat is thoroughly cooked through.

Cotswold Coney Pie

Coney is the Roman name for rabbit, which the invaders brought with them to colonise Britain — and has remained in our hedgerows and wheatfields and shadowy woodlands ever since. The salvation of the nation during the war-time austerity, the rabbit has a special place in our culinary history — and Cotswold Coney Pie, made at Park Farm, Blockley in the North Cotswolds, by Joan and Martin Dee, served dozens of hotels and hospitals until the farm and Martin's television roles left insufficient time for producing the famous pie as a business. I am grateful to them for this recipe.

(Serves 4 heartily)
8 ozs plain flour
6 ozs good lard
juice of ½ lemon
pinch of salt
1 rabbit, jointed and washed in vinegar, then dried
2 onions
seasoning
1 tablesp finely chopped herbs or ½ tablesp if using dried
1 egg, or 1 tablesp milk, to glaze
2 eggs, hardboiled and shelled

Put the rabbit joints and sliced onion to cook gently in just enough water to cover. When tender, remove the rabbit and onion to a deep pie dish, scatter with the herbs, season and pour in the cooking liquid until it reaches the topmost joints, but not to cover the rabbit completely. Slice the eggs and layer on top. Make the pastry by sieving the flour and salt together into a bowl, then cut the lard in small pieces and rub in until crumbly. Mix the lemon juice with cold water and use just enough to make a pliable dough. Roll out lightly into an oblong, then fold the bottom third towards the top and the top third over. Let rest in a cool place for 10 minutes. Roll out into another oblong and repeat the folding process. Again, rest for 20 minutes while you pre-heat the oven to 200°C (Gas Mark 6). Roll the pastry out to fit the top of the dish. Glaze with egg or milk and bake for 25-30 minutes until the pastry is puffed and golden.

Pug's Faggots and Peas

Granny Spencer's grocery shop in Fairford used to have a small passageway at the back, with a long wooden bench on which local folk sat with their jugs waiting for their home-made faggots and peas. The faggots came, with home-grown peas, in rich, slightly spicy gravy and carried home in wide mouthed jugs for the family supper. Friday faggot nights were seasonal, according to the months in which pigs could be slaughtered, and were quite a social interlude: local gossip and such national events as could be gleaned from anyone who had just come in from the Reading Room and caught up with the papers were debated for as long as it took to get the faggots cooked, and the narrow waiting room became known as Pug's Parlour.

1 pig's fry — this is the offal from one pig. heart, liver, meld, etc. (omit the lights for preference). The total weight should be about 2 lbs, but if you cannot get a whole pig's fry, as it is termed, then use 1 lb pig's liver and 1 lb fat pork
1 pig's caul — this is the lacy membrane which encloses the 'fry'
4 onions
1 oz mixed spice (optional)
seasoning
4 ozs breadcrumbs, oatmeal or left-over potatoes
1 flat tablesp finely chopped fresh sage
about 1 tablesp good dripping or pure lard, preferably home-made

Soak the caul in tepid water for about 30 minutes, this will help to open it out then you spread it on a rack to drain. Simmer the washed fry with the thinly sliced onions in a little water for about 40 minutes until tender, drain well then chop all together finely (or you can mince it, but the slightly coarse texture is more traditional). Mix together with the spice (if used), seasoning and breadcrumbs, binding with enough of the cooking liquor to hold the mixture firmly. Cut the caul into 4-inch square pieces and place a spoonful of mixture in the centre of each square. Wrap round neatly and tuck the ends underneath. Place in a deep baking tin, and pour in enough water to come about one-third the way up the faggots, which should be packed close together. Dot with the dripping and bake for about 1-1¼ hours in a pre-heated oven at 180°C (Gas Mark 4), when the faggots should be cooked through.

Put the peas to cook in lightly salted water while you make the gravy. Drain off the excess fat from the faggots. Blend 1 tablespoonful of flour with a little water in a small basin and stir into the baking tin, adding more water as necessary to make sufficient gravy. Stir well to prevent lumps then return to the oven, increasing the heat by a couple of marks — cook for about 15 minutes to thicken the gravy and brown the top of the faggots. They should have a nice dry brown crust on them when cooked to perfection. Drain the peas well and tip into the gravy before serving. It is traditional to serve faggots and peas with thick hunks of bread — not potatoes. (The bread is used, as in the days of old 'trenchers' — to soak up the gravy).

Cotswold Clanger

8 ozs plain flour
4 ozs shredded suet
6 ozs bacon pieces
1 level teasp finely chopped herbs
1 onion
salt and pepper

Mix the flour, a pinch of salt and the suet together with enough cold water to make a firm dough. Turn onto a floured board and press into an oblong shape with your hands — do not roll out like pastry. Chop the bacon and onion into very small pieces and scatter evenly over the suet paste, sprinkle with the herbs and seasoning. Roll up as for roly poly pudding, sealing the edge with water. Place, seal side down, on a well-floured pudding cloth. Tie the short ends tightly with fine string and sew up the long side keeping the cloth fairly loose to give the clanger room to 'plim up'. Place in a large pan of boiling water and keep at a steady boil for about 3 hours, replenishing the water with boiling water to keep the level. Serve hot with good rich gravy and carrots and/or green vegetables. This is very filling so there is no need for potatoes.

Cotswold Feggy Dump

This is the now traditional Christmas pudding — sometimes called plum pudding, when all dried fruits were known collectively as 'plums'. In the Cotswold dialect the fruits are known as 'feggy' often thought to mean figs, but as figs did not feature in the plum pudding it is more likely to mean the dried prunes (also referred to as plums, just for confusion) which were an important addition to the porridge from which it all derived. Plum porridge was a Tudor conception of beef and veal boiled in spices and wine, usually hock or old sack, flavoured with citrus fruits and enriched, when cooked, with fried dried plums and dried grapes, sweetened with honey and thickened with crumbled coarse bread, to be served in a semi-liquid state. The rich pottage later became a filling for pies and in the 18th-century the meat was omitted, and the mixture thickened with a greater proportion of breadcrumbs and solidified with a little flour. The whole was then rolled into a large ball and boiled in a cloth. It was the Victorians who put the Christmas pudding tidily into a basin and covered it with a cloth.

Stir up we beseech Thee, O Lord,
The wills of thy faithful people
That they plenteously bringeth
forth the fruits of good works;
May of Thee be plenteously
rewarded

The Collect for the Sunday before Advent was a timely reminder to the housewives in the congregation to prepare for Christmas, and became popularly known as Stir Up Sunday. This gives the pudding time to mature. Suet has now replaced the original meat, but keeping faith with its origins there is still a good proportion of breadcrumbs used in relation to flour, to keep the pudding light in texture though heavy with fruit. The addition of a grated carrot also makes it more crumbly. Using brown sugar and black treacle darkens the pudding, and with the long boiling the Feggy Dump takes pride of place in the year's cookery calendar.

(Makes a good 1½ lb size pudding)
6 ozs raisins
6 ozs currants
4 ozs shredded suet
2 ozs mixed peel, chopped
4 eggs, beaten
2 ozs plain flour
4 ozs freshly made white breadcrumbs
2 ozs ground almonds
1 level teasp mixed spice
grated rind of 1 lemon
2 tablesps brandy
6 ozs sultanas
2 ozs almonds, flaked and chopped
2 ozs soft brown sugar
2 ozs glacé cherries, rinsed of their sticky coating and chopped in a little flour
1 large carrot, grated
2 level tablesps black treacle

Butter a 2½-pint sized basin. Mix all the ingredients except the eggs and brandy together in a roomy bowl and leave, covered, overnight to allow the flavours to mingle. Add the eggs and brandy, mix — and most importantly wish as you stir — spoon into the basin, pressing down well to pack evenly. Cover with a buttered paper and a cloth. Tie firmly under the basin rim and knot the cloth by bringing the opposite corners together. Boil for 8 hours, making sure that the level of the water is kept up to just below the rim by adding more boiling water to the pan. Remove the cloth and paper. When cold, re-cover with fresh paper, buttered liberally, and tie down with a clean cloth. Keep in a dry cool place (preferably the fridge) until Christmas. The pudding can then be steamed, rather than boiled, for 2 hours Serve with brandy butter and cream.

The tradition of inserting small silver coins or trinkets in the pudding as lucky charms adds that special touch to this special occasion. Wrap them securely in stout greaseproof paper and distribute evenly in the pudding as you pack the mixture into the basin.

Dunch Dump

This dump is steamed — dunch means plain in our language! This recipe comes from an old parish magazine dated 1889 and was contributed by Canon Carbonell. Here it is in his own words.

Scrumptious Pudding

If you have got a steamer (not a sea-going one) try the following pudding:

Take 2 eggs and their weight in flour, sugar and butter. Dissolve 1 teaspoonful of bicarbonate of soda in the eggs; then stir in the flour, sugar and butter. Put 2 tablespoonfuls of any jam in the bottom of a basin large enough to hold twice the quantity (The basin will have to be greased, of course). Leave half the basin to allow for the pudding to swell. Steam it for 2 hours. Don't attempt to boil it, or you will have to give it to the cat!

Ag Pag Dump

A pudding of barley meal, as ground flour was expensive, with leaves and herbs culled from the hedgerows was eaten by country people in the 18th-century. Originally boiled in a cloth tied round in a bundle, the dump (filled with ag-pag, meaning odds and ends of whatever was available) was boiled in the cooking pot suspended over an open fire, along with the hunk of home-cured bacon and a cabbage in its string net.

One teacupful of barley boiled until soft. Wash and chop finely small bunches of washed young nettle tops, dandelion leaves, blackcurrant leaves, watercress, sorrel leaves, a sprig of mint, thyme and sage and a couple of chopped onions, or wood garlic. Beat together with an egg to bind and add a tablespoonful of softened butter. Mould into a ball then place on a floured cloth and boil for about 2 hours.

Spotted Dick

A pudding to conjure up childhood memories.

(Serves 6)
2 ozs currants
2 ozs sultanas
3 ozs caster sugar
8 ozs self-raising flour
4 ozs shredded suet
a large pinch of salt
about ¼ pint water

Put a large pan of water on to boil while making the pudding. Mix the dried fruit with the sugar first to coat it well, then add to the rest of the dry ingredients in a bowl. Add enough water to make a soft, not sticky dough. Turn onto a lightly floured board and gently knead into a plump sausage shape, about 8 inches long. Flour a pudding cloth liberally (this is what gives the spotted dick its creamy smooth coating when cooked). Place the dough in the middle and either sew or pin with two large safety pins along the edge to seal. Tie the short ends tightly with fine string. Boil steadily for about 1½ hours, topping up with more boiling water as necessary. Turn out onto a warmed dish, serve hot, sliced, and sprinkled with caster sugar.

Roly Poly Duff

This is a duff, rather than a dump, because it is baked. If it is boiled, in the same way as spotted dick, then it is a dump!

(Serves 6)
6 ozs self-raising flour
3 ozs shredded suet
pinch of salt
water to mix
about ½ pot jam — raspberry, plum strawberry or blackcurrant — use a good coloured home-made jam

Pre-heat the oven to 220°C (Gas Mark 7). Make the suet crust pastry by mixing the flour, salt and suet together with enough cold water to make a soft dough. Roll out on a floured board to an oblong, roughly 8 x 12 inches. Spread thickly with jam to within 1 inch of the edges. Damp the edges and roll the poly up from the shortest side, pinching the edges to seal in the jam as you go. Place on a greased baking sheet with the join underneath. Brush with a little beaten egg and milk, if liked, to glaze. Bake for about 40 minutes, covering with paper if the crust browns too quickly. Serve hot, sliced, with thin custard.

Midwinter Pie

This lamb and fruit pie takes its name from the medieval sheep merchants of Northleach, from whence this recipe derives. It was from the wealth of the Cotswold fleece in the Middle Ages that the beautiful 'wool' church was built — the wool churches of the Cotswolds are a great legacy of that period.

(Serves 4-6)
8 ozs self-raising flour
4 ozs good lard
pinch of salt
1 egg
1 large or 2 small cooking apples, sliced
1 lb lean lamb, cut into cubes
6 ripe, fresh plums, or prunes, soaked in tea overnight, chopped
½ teasp grated nutmeg
1 oz good dripping
1 level teasp rosemary, finely chopped
1 tablesp sugar

Fry the lamb in the dripping until browned all over. Add the rosemary and nutmeg and leave over a low heat for a further 10 minutes to flavour the meat. Make the pastry by rubbing the lard into the flour, sifted with the salt, until crumbly. Make into a soft, but not sticky dough, with cold water and let rest in a cool place for 20 minutes while pre-heating the oven to 200°C (Gas Mark 6). Line a lightly greased deep pie plate with half the pastry. Place the apple slices on the base, sprinkle the sugar over, then arrange the meat on top. Cover with the chopped plums or prunes. Roll out the remaining pastry and cover over the pie, taking care not to stretch the pastry as it will shrink from the edges during cooking. Seal the edges together with beaten egg. Make a couple of slits on the top to allow the steam to escape. Roll the pastry trimmings into a long thin sausage and twist, like a rope loosely, seal to the outer edge to represent wool skeins. Brush over with the egg and bake for 30-35 minutes until golden brown and the lamb and apples quite tender. Serve with creamed potatoes and a green vegetable.

Matriminy

This is a meat loaf made of pork scraps and the skretchings (the scrumped up morsels of fat left after rendering down lard).

1¼ lbs pork scraps
1 lb skretchings
1¼ lbs stale bread
2½ pints water
1 tablesp salt
½ level teasp ground pepper
1 flat teasp finely chopped parsley
1 onion, chopped
a mean shake of allspice

Soak the bread in the water for 4 hours. Squeeze as dry as possible with your hands and put into a basin. Mince the scraps of pork, the skretchings and the onion into the bread and using a fork mix in well. Add the seasoning, parsley and spice and beat together with a wooden spoon. Press into a well-greased loaf tin and place in a baking tin half filled with warm water. Bake in a pre-heated oven at 180°C (Gas Mark 4) for about 2 hours when the loaf should be browned and firm. Allow to cool in the tin, then turn out onto a serving plate to get quite cold before slicing. If liked, the tin can be lined with rashers of streaky bacon to give an attractive covering to the loaf.

Swell Victorian Headcheese

The head (calf's or pig's) is singed, then soaked in salt water for 24 hours. It is then taken out, scrubbed and cleaned. A red-hot poker is thrust into the ears and nostrils (this sterilises the cavities so is not as barbaric as it sounds!). If the head is overlarge then split it in two into a kettle (a fish kettle) large enough to hold enough water to cover it. Into the kettle put a few bay leaves, a bunch of parsley, a sprig of sage, a sprig of thyme and some summer savoury, two or three onions and a good sized carrot, cut into pieces. In a bag are put some whole cloves, peppercorns and this is added to the other. The meat is then boiled until it drops from the bones. A thin white cloth is placed in a large colander and the meat drained onto it. When quite drained, it is either chopped or picked into fine pieces and packed into a bread bin. Add a very little portion of vinegar to the liquid in which the head was boiled and pour enough of this over the head to mould it. Over the meat place a clean dry cloth and on top of this a weight, say a sadiron or a stone placed on a board.

Gloucestershire Squab Pie

This is what we used to call a 'mag-pag pie' — one made up of leftovers, but very good if you stick to complementary flavours, such as this one of pork with apple and turnip.

(Serves 4)
about 12 ozs cold cooked pork, cut into cubes
½ pint good stock
1 lb potatoes, cooked
1 oz butter or good dripping
4 onions, boiled until soft
3 apples, peeled and sliced
1 turnip (a 'swede-turnip' is best) cooked until soft
a little milk, warmed

Arrange the pork pieces in the bottom of an ovenproof dish. Cover with the onions, season to taste, layer the sliced apple on top then cover with the stock so that it is moist but not swimming in liquid. Mash the potatoes and turnip together with a little warm milk until quite smooth. Pile on top of the pie, covering completely and sealing the edges, fork a pattern on the top to help it crisp. Dot with flakes of butter or dripping and bake at 180°C (Gas Mark 4) for about 1 hour when it should be golden brown and the apple slices tender. Serve with good rich gravy and green vegetables.

Hodge Podge Puddings

This is the Cotswold version of the much favoured North Country Black Puddings — but skinless.

1 quart pig's blood
¼ large loaf, stale
8 ozs barley
4 ozs dry oatmeal
1 quart dried milk reconstituted
1 lb beef suet
8 ozs rice
5 ozs seasoning made up, according to taste, of 7 parts salt, 3 parts pepper, 1 part coriander, 1 part pimento

Cook the rice and barley in enough water to cover until soft. Pour the made-up milk over the bread, then break it up with a fork. Pour the blood over the now soaked bread. Grate the suet into the bowl and add the seasoning. Mix well, beating together with a wooden spoon until well blended. Spoon into a greased, shallow baking tin and bake at 180°C (Gas Mark 4) for about 50 minutes until firm. Allow to get quite cold then cut into squares, or fingers and fry in shallow fat until browned and crisp all over.

Soul Cakes

A soul, a soul, a soul cake,
Please, good Missus, a soul cake,
An apple, pear, plum or cherry,
Or anything to make us merry

The Old Soulers' verse was a kind of begging song that asked for some kind of reward for the Soulers' services of offering prayers for the departed on All Souls' Day, the 2nd of November. It was a Celtic festival, following on from Halloween on the last day of October, and All Saints' Day on the first day of November.

In the Cotswold village of Bisley there is a 13th century Poor Souls' Light in the churchyard —thought to be the only one in England to be outside a church. Inside its carved stone spire, candles were placed for masses to be said for the poor of the parish. It stands on the site of an ancient well head, which became known locally as The Bonehouse. The story is that one dark night a priest was summoned to take the Blessed Sacrament and never reached his destination. Later, his body was found at the foot of the well, and the parish was consequently excommunicated for a period. No burials were allowed in the churchyard, and the dead had to be carried for interment to Bibury — some seven miles away. There is still a corner of the churchyard at Bibury called 'the Bisley Piece'. Soul cakes became the traditional 'reward' to the itinerant Soulers — very much like the mincepie became the customary gift to carol singers who called on the household. As with so many of the cakes devised for festivals which had religious associations, the soul cake is spiced — an echo of the spices brought to the Nativity.

1 lb plain flour
6 ozs caster sugar
6 ozs butter
4 ozs currants
1 level teasp ground mixed spice
3 egg yolks
milk to mix

Beat the butter and sugar together until light and fluffy, then beat in the egg yolks gradually. Sift the flour and spice together into the butter mixture. Beat well, then add the currants with enough milk as necessary to form a soft, but not sticky, dough. Cut into as many pieces as you want the size of each cake and shape into rounds. Place on a greased baking sheet and mark each cake with a cross. Bake in a pre-heated oven at 180°C (Gas Mark 4) for about 15 minutes until risen and golden

Holywake Bake Cake

Holywake is a 17th-century word of the Cotswolds for bonfire, it has its origins in the burning of heretics. As with public hangings, the spectacle attracted an audience and vendors had ready custom for their Holywake Bakes. Later, this parkin type cake had happier associations with village bonfires on Guy Fawkes Night, although, of course, the connotations were as unholy. Origins apart, it is a very good cake for the traditional Bonfire Night, and if made a couple of days in advance it becomes nice and sticky

(Makes 12 pieces)
6 ozs self-raising flour
2 ozs fine oatmeal
1 level tablesp ground ginger
1¼ level teasps bicarbonate of soda
4 ozs raisins
3 ozs brown sugar
¼ pint milk
2 tablesps golden syrup
2 tablesps black treacle
1 egg, beaten
3 ozs butter
icing sugar to dust

Stir the flour, oatmeal, ginger, raisins and bicarbonate of soda together in a bowl. Put the syrup, treacle, butter and sugar to melt slowly over a gentle heat, stir well to blend then pour into the flour mix. Add the egg and beat well. Pour into a greased and lined 10 x 7 inch size tin. Bake in a pre-heated oven at 170°C (Gas Mark 3) for about 1 hour, until firm to the touch, covering with paper if browning too quickly. Allow to cool in the tin, turn out and cut into 12 pieces. Dust with icing sugar just before serving (not before storing otherwise it will sink into the cake).

Dripping Cake

In the days when the family pig was the only meat to sustain the cottagers for months on end, 'butcher's meat', as beef was termed, was a luxury which came into the kitchen on very rare occasions, so home-made dripping was hardly ever available. Many market towns had hostelries which cooked enormous market dinners for the farmers and dealers, at which beef was the centrepiece of a groaning table. Basins of fresh dripping, from the joints, could be bought then at the back door of the hotels and inns for an old sixpence. The thick creamy fat was used for cakes and pastry and when the bottom layer of jellied meat sediment was reached it was a real treat as a spread on hot toast. It still is — and beats all the fancy pots of 'spreads' from the supermarket. Dripping makes a delicious crumbly cake with a texture all its own.

8 ozs self-raising flour
4 ozs caster sugar
6 ozs 'clean' dripping (this means it has no sediment or jelly in the quantity used for the cake)
1 level teasp demerara sugar
6 ozs dried mixed fruit
2 eggs
2 mean shakes of vanilla essence
milk to mix

Rub the dripping into the flour as though making pastry until it is crumbly in texture. Beat in the rest of the ingredients (except the demerara sugar) with enough milk to make a dropping consistency. Spoon into a greased and lined cake tin. Smooth the top and sprinkle the demerara sugar over. Bake in a pre-heated oven at 170°C (Gas Mark 3) for about 1 hour, or until a skewer inserted in the centre comes out clean. Allow to cool in the tin for about 20 minutes before turning out onto a cake rack to get quite cold.

Ampney Apple Cake

The Ampneys are a quartet of small villages; three are famous for the small sharply red cider apples which are peculiar to the Ampneys, the fourth is immortalised as the hymn tune Down Ampney, which Ralph Vaughan Williams composed to honour his Cotswold birthplace. This apple cake is therefore best made with tart, rather than sweet apples, to capture the true taste of the original.

6 ozs self-raising flour
4 ozs butter
1 lb tart apples
3 ozs caster sugar
l egg
3 ozs granulated sugar to sweeten the apple

Stew the apples with very little water until soft, sweeten to taste with the sugar and leave to get cool. Cream the butter and caster sugar together until light and fluffy. Beat in the egg and flour until it is quite stiff. Cut in half and roll out one piece on a well floured board to fit a well greased sandwich tin. Cover with the cold apple, then roll out the remaining cake dough and fit on top. Mark the top into sections and bake in a pre-heated oven at 180°C (Gas Mark 4) for about 1 hour when it should be golden brown and firm to the touch. Leave to cool in the tin and serve dredged with granulated sugar.

Cotswold Honey Toffee

Please to remember the Fifth of November,
Gunpowder, treason and plot.
I see no reason why gunpowder, treason
Should ever be forgot

With traditional toffee, toffee apples, sausages and sticky cake, there is always good reason to remember Guy Fawkes Night with its blazing bonfire lighting up the faces of the children as they tuck into the customary fare.

2 tablesps Cotswold honey
8 ozs granulated sugar
1 oz butter
1 teasp vinegar
1 tablesp water

Put all the ingredients to melt in a pan over a low heat, stir to blend thoroughly then bring to the boil. Keep at a rolling boil without stirring for 10-15 minutes. Test by dropping a spot in cold water, if it is brittle within seconds then it is cooked enough. Remove from the heat and pour into an oiled or buttered shallow tin. Mark into squares when setting, then deeper as it is finally set, which makes it easier to cut or break into pieces when quite cold. Wrap in greaseproof paper and store in an airtight tin if making before Bonfire Night.

Toffee Apples

Toffee apples have been with us since the Middle Ages, when they were sold at fairs and markets, the little apples on wooden sticks being coated with a mixture of beeswax and honey.

(Makes 8 toffee apples)
8 small eating apples
8 wooden sticks
8 ozs soft brown sugar
1 oz butter (unsalted is best)
1 tablesp golden syrup
1 teasp vinegar
5 tablesps water

Dissolve the ingredients together over a gentle heat, stir to blend then bring to the boil and keep at a rolling boil for about 10 minutes until a drop in cold water snaps easily. Have the apples washed and dried ready with the sticks pierced through the centres. Dip each apple into the toffee mixture, twirl it round quickly to coat evenly, then immediately plunge into a bowl of cold water to set the toffee. Shake off the excess water and leave standing upright in bottles to thoroughly set. Cover with cling film or cellophane until needed.

Ciceter Cider

This is an easily made low alcoholic drink as it is not fermented with yeast and is ready to drink in a week, although it does improve its flavour if kept for several months.

3 lbs windfall cooking apples, washed thoroughly and any bad bits cut out
2 lbs granulated sugar
6 quarts cold water
3 really juicy lemons

Cut the apples into small pieces and mince, core and skin as well, into a clean plastic bucket if you haven't an earthenware crock. Pour on the water and leave covered for 7 days, stirring thoroughly every morning and night. Strain into a clean receptacle and stir in the sugar, the juice and finely grated rind of the lemons. Leave to stand for a further 24 hours. Strain into glass bottles with screw tops securely fastened.

Rendering Lard

Cut the inside flear (sometimes called leaf) of fat into evenly sized pieces about ¼ inch square, removing all the skin and bits of lean meat from it. Melt the small pieces of fat over a gentle heat, stirring occasionally. When all the fat has run to clear oil, and the tissues have shrivelled to 'skretchings', tammy through a cheese cloth into bladders (or strain through a muslin-lined sieve into air-tight jars or small basins).

Home-made lard is delicious spread on hot toast, sprinkled with sea salt. Lard to be eaten like this should be put into small china basins and a sprig of rosemary placed on top. Cover with beadweighted muslin covers to be traditional — or cling film and store in a cool place.

The skretchings, the scrumpy morsels of shrivelled up flear were a great treat for the children, sprinkled with coarse sea salt and piled on top of hunks of fresh bread.

War-Time Cream

The austerity of war-time exercised the ingenuity of the Cotswold housewife to vary the basic rations for special occasions. This is one recipe which still has many uses today — try it spread as a base in pastry cases before filling with fresh fruit (the pastry case must be cooked of course).

¼ pint milk
1 level tablesp cornflour
1 level tablesp sugar
2 ozs margarine
3 scant drops of vanilla essence

Slake the cornflour with a couple of spoonfuls of milk until it forms a smooth paste. Boil the remaining milk, stir in the paste, stirring to prevent lumps and let it get quite cold. Beat the margarine and sugar together, with the essence, until pale and fluffy and every trace of sugar granules gone. Now add the cold cornflour mixture a little at a time, whisking well between each addition until it is perfectly smooth and creamy.

December

Traditional Thomasmas and Christmas with Gaufffres, Dumb Cake and Lambswool Tipple to end the year with good cheer

Now thrice welcome, Christmas,
Which brings us good cheer,
Minc'd pies and plum porridge,
Good ale and strong beer;
With pig, goose and capon,
The best that can be,
So well doth the weather
And our stomachs agree

The unknown poet who penned those words captures the traditional festive fare which spells Christmas in all home-lovers' hearts. The custom of going 'A-Thomassing' carried on well into this century in Down Ampney, the small Cotswold village birthplace of Ralph Vaughan Williams. Old Log Book entries record the pupils from the local school taking time off to go to Alex Farm 'AThomassing'. It was a day on which it was customary to beg from the big houses and farms in the neighbourhood for wheat flour to make the Christmas pies, and other goods were equally acceptable in the days when families were large and wages small. Many charities were set to pay out to the poor on St Thomas' Day and became known as St Thomas' Dole; falling on the 21st of December, such alms as were distributed then were particularly welcome to help with Christmas food.

For some families, Christmas fare meant little more than they survived on throughout the year — again, it was often the family pig that was the salvation. Christmas tradition demanded that there should be something a little different, however, and sucking pig became that something special. Originally, keeping a full litter stretched the meagre budget so it was deemed more economical to kill a piglet of about 6 weeks old for the festive feast. The meat is very rich but delicate and soon became a luxury dish rather than a peasant's make-do. The sight of a little piglet roasted whole and served stretched out on a platter with a lemon in its mouth would appear distasteful to some people today — although they would just as cheerfully eat it jointed. However, in keeping with tradition I have included that centuries old centrepiece — a boar's head. A sucking pig is stuffed in much the same way and cooked as for pork, according to weight — dredging it with flour halfway through the cooking time. The Ceremony of Bringing the Boar's Head is still carried out at Christmas-tide at Queen's College, Oxford. Legend gives the origin for the ceremony to the killing of a wild boar by one of the University students, who was completely unarmed except for a copy of Aristotle; when the boar started to attack, the scholarly Copcot thrust Aristotle down its throat, and the boar expired uttering, 'Graecum est'.

The ancient Boar's Head Carol is sung by the College choristers as the decorated boar's head, wreathed in bay and rosemary and with an orange in its mouth, is borne in and placed on the high table.

The Boar's Head in hand bear I,
Bedecked with bays and rosemary,
And I pray you, my masters, by
merry,
Quot estis in convivio
The Boar's Head as I understand,

Is the rarest dish in all this land.
Which thus bedecked with a gay garland
Let us servire cantico

Boar's Head

1 large fresh, or salted, pig's head
oil (for roasting)

for the farce (stuffing):
1 lb pig's liver, minced
brains from the head (optional)
1 onion, finely chopped
2 lbs pork, minced
1 oz butter
1 wineglass of sherry
tongue (from the pig) simmered with bay leaf and peppercorns until tender
1 flat teasp freshly ground black pepper
1 tablesp pistachio nuts, blanched and shredded
level teasp allspice, freshly ground
a mean pinch of bicarbonate of soda

for the decoration:
about ¾ pint glaze made from boiling the bones until jelly-like liquid is produced
1 hard-boiled egg
2 black olives
2 curved sticks of celery
1 small orange
1 red camellia or paper flower
wreath of bay or rosemary

If you give the butcher sufficient time, he will probably bone out the head for you and remove the eyes. The ears should be left on. Thoroughly wash the boned head. Boil the washed bones with half an onion and a carrot, sliced with enough water to cover. Bring to the boil, then simmer for about 1½ hours to extract all the flavour. Remove the bones and vegetables and boil rapidly until the liquid is reduced by half, use for the glaze. It can be coloured with a little caramel or gravy browning, if liked.

Set the oven to 180°C (Gas Mark 4). Make the farce by softening the onion in the butter in a small pan over a low heat. Add to the minced meats, the seasoning and allspice. Skin the tongue, by snipping the underside and peeling off carefully. Dice finely and add to the farce. Moisten with the sherry and mix well together. Lay the boned head, skin down on a working surface. Spread the farce over and sprinkle with the nuts. Re-shape the head and tie it neatly into place with fine string. Brush with oil and roast in a pre-heated oven for about 4 hours, basting with its own juices from time to time.

When cooked and nicely browned, remove carefully onto a dish and press between boards and weights to maintain the shape of the head. Leave overnight to set. Remove the string and brush with the glaze. Leave for several hours for the glaze to set. Cut the egg in half and remove the yolk. Pierce an olive in the centre of each white hollow and attach to the head for eyes. Shape the celery into tusks and position realistically. Serve on a large platter, or silver cake board, raised well up on the table as a centrepiece. Decorate with the red camellia or paper flower behind one ear, a small orange in its mouth, and a garland of bay or rosemary around it.

To carve, start at the back of the head and cut diagonally down the sides of the cheek.

Tomato And Orange Soup

(Serves 4)
2 lbs tomatoes (you can use frozen, or a 1 lb 13 oz tin)
1 onion, sliced
2 pints chicken or vegetable stock
1½ ozs butter
1½ ozs plain flour
1 large orange
2 level tablesps tomato puree
seasoning
4 tablesps cream

Cut the tomatoes over a sieve so that the juice drips through into a large pan and you can remove the pips by catching them in the sieve as you chop the tomatoes into pieces. Put the onion, stock and seasoning with the tomatoes and the thinly pared rind of half the orange into the pan. Bring just to the boil, reduce to simmering point and cook gently for 30 minutes. Rub through a sieve. Melt the butter in the hot pan and make a smooth paste with the flour by adding a little of the soup. Gradually stir in the soup and add the purée. Bring again to the boil and cook for 1 minute. Stir in the juice from half the orange, add a spoonful of sugar (optional) and the seasoning, do not allow to boil again. Warm through at the point of serving and pour into soup dishes. Garnish with a spoonful of cream swirled through and the rest of the orange thinly sliced floating on the top.

Traditional Turkey

(Serves 8 with enough for a cold dish later)
12 lbs turkey, dressed weight
1 lb cooking apples
2 ozs caster sugar
4 ozs butter
8 medium size eating apples
2 lbs chestnuts, peeled
½ pint milk
12 ozs pork sausagemeat
seasoning
parsley to garnish

Pre-heat the oven to 175°C (Gas Mark 4). Wipe the turkey thoroughly and lightly season with pepper and salt. Boil the chestnuts in the milk for 1 minute, reduce the heat and cook slowly for a further 20 minutes. Drain and chop. Cook the prepared 1 lb of apples with the sugar and 1 tablespoonful of water. When soft, put into a mixing bowl with the sausagemeat and chestnuts, seasoning lightly. Add 1 oz of butter and beat until well blended. Reserve 4 tablespoons of the mixture and stuff the rest into the turkey. Secure the stuffing inside the bird by sewing or by a skewer to close the opening. Spread the rest of the butter over the turkey. Roast for about 4 hours, basting quite often. An hour before it is ready to serve, prepare the 8 apples. Wash and core them, then split the skins in about 6 places vertically — when the skins split during cooking they will then fall away from the apple in a petal shape. Stuff the centre of each apple with the remaining stuffing and place a flake of butter on top. Cook on the bottom shelf round the turkey, garnished with parsley.

Venison With Wine And Thyme

The majority of the great country houses had deer parks attached to their extensive grounds, ensuring a plentiful supply of venison, which had been the royal preserve since the Norman Conquest. It was customary in many manorial estates to present the tenants with a joint of venison when they paid the Christmas rent. It was a meat much favoured by the Romans, who served it with dates and damsons and sauces. The Elizabethans favoured the spices and herbs, but marinating it in wine and roasting it with rashers across its back was the gourmet dish created at the turn of the century. The saddle is the prime cut, and as venison is now more freely available in the shops it is well worth recreating those days of fullbodied tastes.

(Serves 12)
1 saddle of venison
10 rashers of streaky bacon
4 fl ozs red wine (port if available)

Marinade:
½ pint red wine
½ pint red wine vinegar
½ pint water
1 sprig of fresh thyme
4 juniper berries, crushed
3 bay leaves, crumbled
1 blade of mace, crumbled
a sliver of orange peel,
remove all the white pith

Trim the meat of any hard skin then place in a dish where it is almost completely enclosed. Mix all the marinade ingredients together, adding more water if necessary to completely cover it. Cover with muslin or a cloth, but not a lid as it must have air, leave in a cold place to marinate for 2 days, turning it over at least twice a day.

Drain and pat dry. Tie the rashers across the saddle with fine string and place in a baking tin. Cover loosely with foil and roast in a pre-heated oven at 200°C (Gas Mark 6) for 30 minutes. Baste with the marinade and reduce the temperature to 180°C (Gas Mark 4) to cook for a further hour, continue basting during this time and keeping covered with the foil as venison has a tendency to dry out quickly. Pour the port wine into the roasting tin to strengthen the marinade during this last cooking time. Remove the foil, and cut off the rashers — reserving them for the garnish by rolling them immediately while still warm. Increase the oven temperature back to 200°C (Gas Mark 6) and return the joint to brown the skin for another 10 minutes. Remove onto a warmed serving dish. Strain the juices and thicken for gravy, if liked.

Serve with redcurrant jelly and game chips to be truly traditional.

Roast Duck with Cherries and Celery

(Serves 4-6)
4 lbs duck, dressed weight
1 tin cherries
1 head celery
2 ozs butter
2 tablesps vegetable oil
½ pint good stock
bouquet garni
watercress or parsley to garnish
seasoning

Set oven to 175°C (Gas Mark 4). Prepare duck and season. Melt the butter and oil together in a large pan and fry the duck for about 10 minutes, turning to brown evenly. Remove and place in a roasting tin. Prepare the celery and cut into even-sized strips and fry in the remaining fat. Drain well and keep to one side. Add the bouquet garni and stock to the duck. Cover and roast for about 1 hour or until just cooked. Drain the cherries and add, with the celery sticks, to the duck; cook, uncovered, for a further 15 minutes. Remove onto a hot serving dish, arranging the celery and cherries around the duck, and garnish with watercress or parsley.

Pork with Cider Sugared Apples

(Serves 4-6)

4 ½ lbs loin of pork, with skin on
1 pint dry cider
8 eating apples
1 teasp red food colouring
3 tablesps vegetable oil
6 ozs granulated sugar
salt
sprigs of parsley

Ask the butcher to chine the joint and score the skin. Pre-heat the oven to 175°C (Gas Mark 4). Brush the skin with the oil and sprinkle with salt to make a nice crisp crackling. Cook for 2-2½ hours. Prepare the garnish about 30 minutes before serving. Peel and core the apples. Dissolve the sugar in the cider over a low heat, then bring to the boil, add the colouring and reduce the heat. Poach the apples gently in the cider syrup until they are tender and nicely pink but still whole — about 15-20 minutes. Remove the apples to a plate. Boil the syrup rapidly to reduce to about half the quantity, pour over the apples and leave to set. Serve the pork on a warmed dish, surrounded by the sugared apples with a sprig of parsley on top of each.

Golden Christmas Pudding

This is a light version of the traditional heavy-fruited pudding, and is delicious served with Golden Sauce. The pudding will keep in a cool place for a couple of weeks, so can be made a little in advance of Christmas Day.

(Serves 6)
4 ozs margarine
2 ozs glace cherries, chopped
3 eggs, beaten
4 ozs sultanas
6 ozs self-raising flour
2 ozs dried apricots, chopped fine
3 ozs soft brown sugar
1 oz ground almonds
1 orange
2 tablesps sweet sherry

Prepare a steamer. Grease a 1½-pint size pudding basin and a double sheet of greaseproof paper. Put the chopped apricots in a small basin with the sherry and leave for 15 minutes to start absorbing it. Beat the margarine and sugar together until fluffy. Add the eggs, a little at time, beating well between. Stir in the fruit, ground almonds, the grated rind of the orange (reserve the rest for the sauce), and the apricots. Save the sherry. Mix well then fold in the flour. Turn the mixture into the prepared basin, cover with the greaseproof paper, making a pleat on the top to allow for the pudding to rise. Tie on a pudding cloth and steam for 2 hours. When cooked remove the cloth and paper at once, pour over the sherry, then when quite cold replace with clean greased paper and cloth. Tie down ready to steam for a further hour on Christmas Day.

Golden Sauce

2 ozs butter
1 egg
the juice of 1 orange
4 ozs icing sugar, sifted
1 tablesp sweet sherry

Separate the egg and put the yolk with the sherry, juice, butter and icing sugar in a basin over a pan of simmering water. Stir over a gentle heat until thickened — about 10 minutes. Remove from the heat. Whisk the egg white until stiff, fold in the sherry sauce carefully and serve warm and foaming.

Tipsy Trifle

This is the real thing — Victorian type custard (rather than bright yellow custard powder) and tipple soaked fruit. For delicate grannies and precocious off-spring, substitute the tipple for pure fruit juice.

(Serves 8)
1 round of home-made Victoria sponge (or ½ pkt of trifle sponges)
4 tablesps home-made sloe gin or wine or sherry or fruit juice
about 8 ozs fruit — sliced bananas, slowly thawed frozen strawberries or raspberries, orange segments, or a mixture of fresh, rather than tinned fruit — put into a small bowl with the tipple to steep
1 pint milk
small vanilla pod
5 eggs
2 tablesps caster sugar
4 ozs crushed macaroons
½ pint whipping cream
Flaked and toasted almonds to decorate

Put the milk and vanilla pod to heat, but do not bring to the boil. Let the pod infuse for 15 minutes while the milk cools, it can then be removed, wiped and stored for use again. Beat 3 eggs and the yolks of the other 2 together, strain onto the milk, add the sugar and cook over a very gentle heat, stirring until the custard thickens. Do not allow to boil. Remove from heat and sprinkle surface with a little granulated sugar to stop a skin forming. While the custard is cooling, take your prettiest glass dish and break up the sponge cake to layer in the bottom. Strain the tipple from the fruit carefully and spoon it over the sponge so that it is well soaked. Now arrange the fruit over then layer the macaroons on top. Stir the cooled custard and pour carefully over the whole trifle. Leave to chill. Whip the cream until bulky, spread just over half all over the top to mask the custard. Continue whipping the remaining cream until stiff enough to pipe rosettes around the edge. Scatter with the almonds. Serve well chilled.

Everlasting Syllabub

This is an Elizabethan dish, very easy to make and quite delicious. The following is a receipt dated 1671 and gives the original version of milking the cow into the wine or cider.

Take a pint of verjuice (crab-apple juice — the fore-runner of our cider). milk the cow into the verjuice; take off the curd (when it sours). Take the sweetcream and beat it together with a little sherry and sugar. Put it in your syllabub pot, then strew with sugar and send it to table.

(Serves 6)
¼ pint white wine
2 tablesps lemon juice
2 level teasps finely grated lemon rind
10 fl ozs fresh double cream
3 ozs caster sugar

Put the wine with the sugar and lemon rind and juice in a shallow bowl and leave to infuse for 6 hours. Stir well then add the cream, tip into a mixing bowl and whip until the mixture is softly stiff and holds its shape. Do not overwhip otherwise it may curdle or separate. Spoon into 6 long glasses. Chill.

Cider Syllabub

¼ pint dry cider
3 level tablesps caster sugar
10 fl ozs double cream
1 orange

Steep the grated rind, and juice of the orange with the sugar and cider for at least 3 hours. Whip the cream until it is bulky and will hold its shape. Fold in the cider mixture to preserve the bulk. If it starts to thin down, then whip it all together until it regains a stiff texture —taking care not to overwhip. Spoon into glass dishes to serve. Chill for at least 30 minutes.

Game Chips

These are thinly cut potato chips deep-fried and, as their name implies, served traditionally with game.

(Serves 4)
1 lb potatoes, peeled
oil for deep-frying
sea salt and freshly ground black pepper for seasoning

Slice the potatoes very thinly, using a mandolin if you have one. Soak in cold water for 30 minutes to remove the excess starch then drain well and dry on a cloth, or kitchen paper. Heat the oil in a deep pan until a cube of bread dropped in turns brown as you count to 40. Lower the chips in carefully and stir them around a bit to stop them sticking together. They should take about 5 minutes to brown and crisp to perfection. If there are too many to cook all at once, remove the cooked chips and keep warm, uncovered under a moderate grill while you cook the rest. Sprinkle liberally with sea salt and a shake of pepper. Serve at once.

Game Pie

Hot water crust:
1 lb plain flour
pinch of salt
1 egg yolk
6 ozs best lard
¼ pint boiling water, if a softer crust is preferred use half milk

Filling:
1 pheasant, grouse or partridge, dressed
1 hare, dressed
1 onion
½ lb pie, veal or lean pork
½ pint good bone stock
½ lb sausagemeat
½ lb streaky rashers, derinded
½ oz gelatine
1 egg
½ teasp each of finely chopped parsley, thyme and marjoram and sage
a shake each of salt, pepper and allspice

Joint the game bird of choice and the hare, put them in a pan and cover meanly with water, bring just to the boil, remove any scum which rises and simmer until the meat is tender.

Make the hot water crust by putting the flour, sifted with the salt into a large bowl. Drop the egg yolk into the centre. Boil the water and lard together and pour while still bubbling into the centre of the flour. Beat well with a wooden spoon until pliable and cool enough to knead with the fingers until quite smooth. Cover with a cloth and rest in a warm place for 20 minutes. It must not get cold. Roll out carefully but not too thinly and line a greased pie tin and lid if using a proper mould.

To raise a pie without using a mould:
Cut off a quarter of the dough. Roll out the remainder and place a well floured jar in the centre. Draw the outer circle up the sides of the jar, moulding smoothly with the fingers to the required height. Tie a double thickness of greased paper round the dough wall then stand it on a baking sheet before removing the jar by giving a sharp twist. Fill with the meat and roll out the rest of the dough to fit as a lid, sealing the edges with water and pinching together. You can get an accurate shape and size for the lid by using the base of the jar as a guide. A loose-bottomed cake tin will also serve as a pie mould.

Filling:
Cut all the flesh into pieces not larger than 2 inches. Mix the sausagemeat and the finely chopped onion and sage together and form into 8 small balls. Roll the rashers round the sausagemeat balls and place in the base of the pie round the edge. Pack pieces of meat in between, then fill the pie, sprinkling the seasoning and spice and herbs between the layers. Break the egg up with a fork and brush inside the rim, sealing to the pie by pinching the edges. Crimp into a pattern and make leaf shapes from the remaining pastry. Make a hole in the top to allow the steam to escape, then glaze with the rest of the egg. Bake at 200°C (Gas Mark 6) for 30 minutes, reduce the heat to 170°C (Gas Mark 3) and cook for a further 1½ hours, covering the top with paper if browning too quickly. Dissolve the gelatine in ½ pint good bone stock and when almost at setting point pour into the pie very carefully through the hole in the lid of the cooked and cooled pie. Pour the remaining jelly onto a cold plate to set, to serve chop with a wet knife (to make it sparkle) and arrange around the pie. Allow a good 6 hours for the pie jelly to set completely, so it is better to make the pie the day before it is needed.

Christmas Cake

9 ozs plain flour
12 ozs sultanas
2 ozs candied peel
2 ozs almonds, chopped
8 ozs soft brown sugar
1 teasp mixed spice
1 full tablesp black treacle
12 ozs raisins
12 ozs currants
4 ozs glace cherries, chopped
8 ozs butter
4 eggs, lightly beaten
pinch of salt
2 tablesps brandy

Grease and line an 8-inch cake tin with well-greased greaseproof paper. Tie a double band of brown paper 1 inch higher than the rim round the outside of the tin. Pre-heat the oven to 150°C (Gas Mark 2) Cream the butter and sugar until pale and light. Add the egg gradually, beating well, then the treacle. Sieve the flour, salt and spice together and stir in with the fruit. Mix thoroughly. Spoon into the prepared tin and bake for 3 hours, reduce the heat slightly for another hour or until a skewer comes out quite clean, covering the top with paper if browning too quickly. Leave cake to cool in the tin for 15 minutes before turning out carefully on a rack. Before it is quite cold, turn upside down, pierce the bottom several times with a skewer and dribble in the brandy.

When completely cold, wrap in

greaseproof paper, then foil, and store in an airtight tin until ready to cover with almond paste and royal icing.

Almond Paste

8 ozs icing sugar, sifted
8 ozs ground almonds
1 egg
2 teasps lemon juice

Mix the almonds and sugar together. Lightly whisk the egg and add the lemon juice, then add this to the dry ingredients using a wooden spoon until a stiff paste is formed. Knead on a board sprinkled with icing sugar and roll out to fit the top of the cake. This quantity is sufficient to make a band of paste to go round the cake as well, if required. If not, reserve it to stuff dates as a sweetmeat.

To cover the cake, brush the top first with either lightly whipped egg white, or 1 tablespoon of apricot jam warmed with 1 tablespoon of water, to enable the almond paste to stick firmly on top.

Chocolate Yule Log

The bringing home of the yule log signifies Christmas and the chocolate cake replica of it on the tea-table is now one of the traditions of the celebration fare.

2 heaped tablesps plain flour
3 eggs
3 ozs caster sugar
2 heaped teasps cocoa
small pinch of salt

Filling:
3 ozs butter
6 ozs icing sugar, sifted
1 level dessertsp cocoa
2 tablesps water

Pre-heat the oven to 200°C (Gas Mark 6). Grease and line a swiss roll tin. Whisk the eggs and sugar in a bowl over a pan of warm water until creamy. Remove from the heat. Whisk again until cool and a ribbon trail is left on the surface when a little of the mixture is shaken from the whisk. Fold in the flour, salt and cocoa (which should be sifted together). Spread evenly in the tin and bake for 10 minutes when the sponge should be springy to the touch. Turn onto greaseproof paper. Trim the edges if they have crisped too much. Roll up with the greaseproof paper inside. Cool on a wire rack. Make the butter icing filling by beating the butter with the icing sugar and water until light and fluffy, then add the cocoa and beat again. Unroll the sponge and spread the filling over to within half an inch of the edges, using about a quarter of the filling for this. Place the log on a plate with the join side underneath. Spread the rest of the chocolate butter icing all over the log, make a few swirly lines to represent bark then decorate with a sprig of holly.

Pickwickian Mince Pies

(Makes about 18)
4 ozs butter
1 egg, beaten
4 ozs caster sugar
8 ozs self-raising flour
1 lb mincemeat
2 tablesps brandy (optional)
pinch of salt
icing sugar to dust

This is a shortcake textured pastry so beat the sugar and butter together until soft and creamy. Add 2 tablespoons of the flour, then the egg, beat well. Add the rest of the flour and form a soft dough. Cover and chill for 30 minutes. Pre-heat the oven to 175°C (Gas Mark 4). Grease deep patty tins. Roll out the pastry on a floured board and cut out rounds with a pastry cutter. Line the tins and fill with mincemeat. Top with the rest of the pastry rolled out and cut out for 'lids'. Seal the edges with water and pinch to close. Cut a wide cross on top of each pie and pull the points back a little, this will allow the steam to escape. Bake for 25-30 minutes until cooked and golden. Cool on a wire tray. Store in an airtight tin. When ready to serve, warm the pies gently and warm the brandy in a metal ladle. Ignite the warmed brandy and while still smoking dribble a little in the cut of each pie. Dredge with icing sugar and serve immediately.

Gloucestershire Gauffres

(Makes 24)
2 ozs butter
2 ozs golden syrup
2 ozs plain flour
2 ozs caster sugar
1 level teasp ground ginger, or nutmeg
½ pint double cream
1 scant tablesp brandy

Well butter 2 baking sheets and pre-heat the oven to 160°C (Gas Mark 3). Melt the butter, syrup and sugar in a small pan until liquid. Sift the flour and spice together and stir into the butter mixture. Spoon small blobs onto the baking sheets, spaced well apart. Bake for about 10 minutes until golden brown. Allow to cool just enough to handle. Remove each gauffre with a spatula individually and wrap quickly round the handle of a wooden spoon, then ease off and pinch together one end, leaving the other open, like a brandy snap. As you ease it off the handle give the closed end a little tap down on a board to flatten it so that the gauffre stands upright when filled. Keep warm while working otherwise they become too brittle to roll around the handle properly. Fill, when cold, with the cream whipped with the brandy. Serve in a small basket.

Dumb Cakes

These cakes got their curious name from the custom of being made in absolute silence by the unmarried ladies of the Cotswolds, who were anxious to find some sign of whom their intended was to be. On Christmas Eve, the Cotswold lasses would make their cakes without speaking to anyone at all during their making, as this would break the magic spell they were stirring into them. They would then scratch their initials on the top and leave them to bake in the ashes of the fire as they went to bed. The front door would be left open and at midnight a suitor would enter and prick his initials on the top of the cake beside the girl's. On Christmas Day, if the maiden ate the dumb cake with the initials on — again in silence — it was a sign that she accepted the rather quaint proposal! Unfortunately there appears to be no record of what the cakes contained, and it is very difficult to imagine how the initials remained legible if they were only scratched in. However, this cake is a nice plain one, in contrast to the rich fruit of the Christmas cake, and contains almonds because they are mentioned in Genesis — so appropriately connected with the Scriptures to warrant a place on the Christmas table.

6 ozs butter
4 ozs caster sugar
2 eggs, beaten

2 ozs ground almonds
4 ozs self-raising flour
4 ozs icing sugar
2 tablesps milk
a few drops of almond essence
toasted flaked almonds

Grease and line the base of a loaf tin. Pre-heat the oven to 170°C (Gas Mark 3). Beat 4 ozs of the butter and the caster sugar together until light. Add a couple of drops of essence, then beat in the eggs a little at a time. Fold in the flour and ground almonds, then the milk. Spoon into the tin and bake for 45-50 minutes until light golden in colour and firm to the touch. Cool on a wire tray. Beat the rest of the butter and the icing sugar together with a drop of essence until smooth. Pipe a swirly line down the centre of the cake and spike with the flaked almonds.

Royal Fudge

Her Royal Highness, The Princess of Wales, kindly donated this recipe for a fund-raising collection of recipes to celebrate the centenary of Fairford Cottage Hospital, the smallest hospital in Gloucestershire, the home of the royal family. It is so good, and one of the simplest to make and I am delighted that Her Royal Highness agreed to its inclusion here for all Cotswold cooks to share. Small boxes of this creamy fudge make ideal personal gifts for special friends at Christmas.

2 ozs butter
1 lb granulated sugar
4 tablesps water
large tin sweetened, condensed milk

Put the butter, sugar and water into a large saucepan, (preferably a non-stick saucepan). Stir gently until the sugar has dissolved. Add the condensed milk and bring to the boil. Simmer on a very low heat until the mixture thickens and browns — this should take about 30 minutes. Stir occasionally during simmering. Remove from the heat and beat well. Pour into a greased tray. Wait until it is set and then cut into squares.

Light Wine Punch

This is a nice, refreshing punch, served chilled.

1 bottle white wine
1 bottle light soda water
3 oranges
1 lemon
3 sprigs of mint
3 tablesps caster sugar

Mix all the ingredients together, add in the mint sprigs last. Chill thoroughly and serve in frosted glasses. To frost glasses: lightly whip the white of an egg in a saucer. Dip the rim of the glass into the egg white, then plunge into caster sugar, twisting the glass to coat evenly. Shake off any excess sugar and leave to dry and harden before using.

Cotswold Lambswool

This is a wassail — with the addition of pulped apples to symbolise the gossamer light wool from the Cotswold lambs on whose backs the wealth of the region — and indeed the country — once rested. The Chancellor of the Exchequer realised this and chose a woolsack for his seat of office in respect of the old adage:

In Europe the finest wool is English.
In England the finest wool is Cotswold.

(Serves 8)
2 pints brown ale
½ pint dry sherry or white wine
6 small cooking apples
3 ozs soft brown sugar
strip of lemon peel
1 stick of cinnamon
½ level teasp grated nutmeg
½ level teasp ground ginger

Wash the apples, slit the skin round the middle and bake until cooked and fluffy. Remove from the oven and when cool enough to handle, remove the skins and scrape the pulp away from the cores. Put into the bottom of the bowl in which you are going to serve the lambswool. Put the rest of the ingredients in a large pan and heat through, do not allow to boil. When really hot pour over the apple pulp and stir through so that it floats on the top. Ladle into heated glasses and toast one another in the way the old farming Saxons did when they tilled the rich red soil of our hills and wolds and lived the good Cotswold life — *Ves heill*: 'Good Health'.

Whisky Mincemeat

Make this early in December so that the flavours have time to mingle before using for special mincepies.

(Makes 3 lbs)
12 ozs raisins
6 ozs currants
4 ozs soft brown sugar
4 ozs shredded beef suet
3 tablesps whisky (use brandy or rum if preferred)
2 small cooking apples, peeled and chopped fine
1 orange
1 lemon
1 level teasp mixed spice

Put the dried fruit in a bowl and mix in the sugar to coat. Add the suet, the chopped apples, then grate the rinds of the orange and lemon into it, stir well. Squeeze out the juice and add to the mixture. Sprinkle the spice over then stir in the whisky. Mix well and leave covered for an hour. Give the mincemeat another stir then pack into clean dry jars. Cover with waxed discs and seal down. Store in a dry, dark place.

Brandy Butter

The traditional partner to Christmas pudding — try, also a small spoonful popped under the lid of hot mince pies. Try it as a luxurious butter cream icing for piping on cakes.

4 ozs butter, softened
4 ozs icing sugar, sifted
4 ozs caster sugar
1 tablesp milk
1 tablesp brandy

Beat the butter with a wooden spoon until it is very light. Gradually beat in the sugars, alternately with the milk and brandy. Use immediately for piping, or pile into a pretty pot for serving with hot puddings. This will keep for a week in the fridge.

Index

Snacks and Supper Dishes

Cakes, Bread and Biscuits

Sweets and Drinks

Sauces and Preserves

Notes

Also from Sigma:

Traditional Derbyshire Fare

300 recipes plus the stories and anecdotes behind them

Jill Armitage

Some Derbyshire dishes are well known, like the Bakewell Pudding; many more, including some of the most delectable, are little known outside the places whose name they bear. The recipes are individual, easy, economical, with readily available ingredients, and have a strong regional accent.
This is Derbyshire food at its best.

About the Author:
Jill Armitage is a lifetime resident of Derbyshire; a trained photojournalist with thousands of articles and dozens of books to her credit. Jill and her husband owned a hotel with a renowned restaurant in Bakewell where she was responsible for buying local, seasonal produce and working on recipes for their discerning clientele.

£12.99

All of our books are available through booksellers. For a free catalogue, please contact:

Sigma Leisure, Stobart House, Pontyclerc. Penybanc Road, Ammanford SA18 3HP

Tel: 01269 593100 Fax: 01269 596116

info@sigmapress.co.uk

www.sigmapress.co.uk